D1231454

Peanut's Legacy

DAFNA MICHAELSON JENET

MOtivational PRESS®
LEADERS IN GLOBAL PUBLISHING

Published by Motivational Press, Inc.
1777 Aurora Road
Melbourne, Florida, 32935
www.MotivationalPress.com

Manufactured in the United States of America.

ISBN: 978-1-62865-442-4

Contents

For Peanut's Daddy,
Michael.
Without you I could not heal.
I love you with all of my heart
and all of my soul.

I long to feel your soft skin

I long to feel the weight of you in my arms

As I rock you to sleep at night

I long to feel the magic of nursing you

Intimately, rhythmically

I long to see you gazing into your Daddy's eyes

I long to see your first smile

Your first laugh

Your first giggle

I long to hear the word mama from your lips

I yearn for you with each baby I see on the street

I mourn you with every milestone we miss

I carry you with me in my deepest thoughts

Every prayer I utter includes you inside

With each butterfly that passes

I know you were here

I know you are still here

Peanut,

I love you,

I miss you

Foreword

There are some parts of life that are really tough. Losing a baby is really tough. Losing at baby at any stage of pregnancy is really tough. For most people, the moment you have a positive pregnancy test, one's thoughts quick turn to "what is my due date?", "what season will I be pregnant in?" then quickly pivots to "what color hair will my baby have?", "will my baby look like me?", "will my child have the talents of my partner?" and then for some, you lose the baby. The initial shock is so painful; followed by the reality of the loss. It is so hard to think about the lost potential of this future child.

Miscarriage rates range from 18 to 80% depending on maternal age. Miscarriage rates increase with mom's age. 40% of pregnancies at age 40 end in loss. Do I tell patients this at their first prenatal visit when the pregnancy is progressing normally? No. If a mom asks, I usually provide a miscarriage range applicable to their specific situation, and try not to dwell on that when things are progressing well. 50% of miscarriages over all gestational ages are due to chromosomal abnormalities. Chromosomal abnormalities occur at the time of conception and there is no way to modify that risk. This fact makes pregnancy loss so difficult to cope with. We, physician and patients, can't do anything to help decrease that risk.

Dafna, the author, asked what is my process for dealing with loss? For me personally in my pregnancies, I remained very guarded until my baby was on the fetal monitor about to deliver. I didn't let myself get excited about having a baby, I didn't buy baby clothes or decorate the baby's room until after delivery. However, this was my choice, this is what was best for me personally given all the pregnancy complications that I was aware of and have experienced with my patients. I don't really think this is a normal response to pregnancy and I certainly try to be less guarded for my patients. For my patients, I am less apprehensive and more hopeful especially after 20 weeks of pregnancy and for my "high risk" patients, I remain cautiously optimistic through the entire pregnancy.

Personally and professionally, I feel that close family/partners/spouses and other women with similar experience provide the best comfort at this time of loss. For others, support from their community, such as a faith organization or work community, can be beneficial. Some patients are open with their work colleagues and others prefer more privacy, both of which are normal responses. In general, I find that most work places are not particularly supportive as institutions in regards to leave policies for pregnancy loss for either partner, or for maternity leave. Stronger advocacy for policies for support of families would be beneficial for all.

Another aspect of pregnancy loss that I find painful is the way that the field of obstetrics and gynecology is organized. We do our best to help patients avoid triggers to aggravating their grief at any follow up visits but somethings are hard to change- you have the same physician, you sit in the same waiting room and the same exam room, you see other pregnant women in the hallway, you hear a Doppler heartbeat thru office walls for example. I try so hard to arrange the next visit in a different room but there are so many aspects of the visit that can't be controlled. It is so hard to see your physician for "recurrent pregnancy loss- ie multiple miscarriages" or "infertility-trouble conceiving" when the waiting room seems like it is packed with lots of happy pregnant moms. The sub specialty of family planning is even worse, doctors trained in dealing with later losses or taking care of patients with babies with complex abnormalities sitting next to patients making different choices. I would like my patients to always know that I am thinking about them in these difficult times and trying to make the office environment easier to cope with.

Hopefully, as patients, physicians, including obstetrician gynecologists talk more and write more and we open up to family, friends, close and sometimes not so close acquaintances, the heartache of miscarriage will decline with time. Everyone grieves differently but hopefully by providing more resources online, in the community, and in our neighborhoods, such as this personal story, it will help ALL with all types of pregnancies that end too too soon.

Lesley N. Bevan, MD

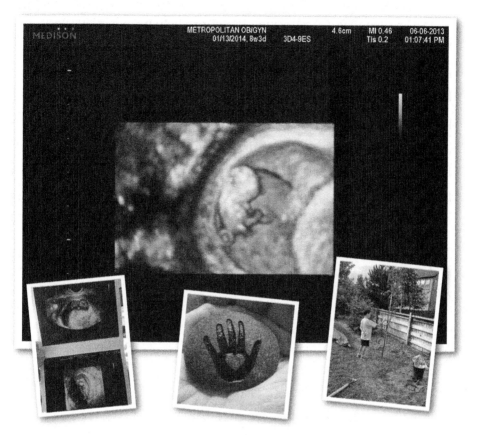

The Peanut Project

In memory of our baby that did not make it, and in honor of the women and families who follow on the painful path of fetal demise

At 20 weeks pregnant, my dreams and plans took a devastating turn. In the matter of a few hours I was no longer carrying a baby. The world became a very bleak place for my husband and I.

As I reflect upon all that has happened and what my family needed that we did not know how or who to ask for, I've learned that perhaps my baby's very short existence does not need to be in vain.

Peanut

A story with an unintended ending

TUESDAY, JUNE 11TH

I'm pregnant! And 40...

When I found out I was pregnant the first thing I did was run to the computer and begin searching for sites that were geared towards women pregnant in their 40's. OK, that's not entirely true. The day went a little more something like this.

It was the Monday after Mother's Day. My husband had decided that one day was not enough and we had celebrated all weekend. I was pampered: my husband/kids/chefs prepared my favorite meals, and we had picnicked on the great lawn of the Botanic Gardens. It was everything I could have hoped for and I was wiped out and filled with love. Sunday night I'd had a pretty restless night sleep and some weird dreams. I often wake up before 5:30 and curse my age for no longer letting me experience the sleep-in phenomenon. I mean it must be the age causing my sleeplessness as opposed to stressing about finances or my kids or my spouse's happiness, right? But I digress... (Early pregnancy brain symptoms I wonder?) I was lying there in bed and thinking how nice it would be to roll over and share some intimacy with my spouse. An early morning guilty pleasure... I knew it was little more than a pipe dream. Within minutes the rigamarole of getting the kids up, showered and dressed, fed, bags packed and out the door while simultaneously dressing, showering and feeding ourselves would make the aforementioned lovely thought impossible. I sighed to myself and then realized, when was the last time I had a period?

As any good woman of the internet age would do, I rolled over, picked up my phone and opened my Pink Pad period tracker app. Much to my chagrin, all the data had been wiped due to a series of unfortunate events with my phone. (Another rant for another day.) I began trying to visualize the last time I'd inserted a tampon. I know, I know TMI. Generally when I'm trying to remember, I can think of times when I was uncomfortable and had to slide the tampon up my sleeve for some semblance of privacy en route to the ladies' room. I was drawing a complete blank. Not one recollection. That damn age thing again.

Then it occurred to me. I'd traveled to Las Vegas soon after my husband's birthday. I had joined him while he was on a conference. I had left early to take care of the kids, and I vaguely recollected uncomfortably maneuvering a tampon insertion in the not-so-spacious confines of the airplane bathroom. My best guess was that was the last time I had seen my monthly visitor.

I opened the calendar app. I began to count. I stopped breathing. It had been exactly 6 weeks, 42 days, since my last period. I've been a 28-day cycle girl darn near my whole life. Clockwork regularity. I knew I was either pregnant or menopause had begun.

My husband and I are blessed with three children. And yes, even with all the drama and trauma of our wonderful offspring, I mean blessed. One from his first marriage, 2 from mine. We recently celebrated our 2nd anniversary. Without trying to jinx it or whatever, I can honestly say this time around we both got it right. He is the partner I have always dreamed of. You can write it off to be honeymoon-phase thinking if you like, but let me remind you: we have three children. There was no honeymoon. I dreamt of having a child with him. I knew the inherent risks. I also knew that we were within, if not spitting distance, of our children reaching a very comfortable level of independence. The oldest has just graduated high school and is beginning his adulthood.

My body ached to be with child, with his child.

We talked about it. I tried to resign myself to shut down those thoughts. We talked some more. We agreed to give it a try. I was on cloud 9! I immediately booked an appointment with an OB. She said I looked good and we could go for it. I ran out to buy the best prenatal vitamins I could find.

Beyond the age element, I felt a serious urgency. About one year prior I had discovered lumps in my breasts. After genetic testing revealed that my percentage of breast cancer risk was in the 90's I decided to undergo a pre-emptive strike and had both of my breasts removed. At that same time, I was advised that my family history, which I had just learned included ovarian cancer, raised additional cancer risks to the point that a hysterectomy and oophorectomy were also advised, if not right away then at the first signs of menopause. The shop would be closed. I opted to wait.

The night I came home from the OB appointment my husband and I, like giddy teenagers with a secret, began referring to our current situation as "peanut season". I downloaded apps to use to track my fertile days and we gave it a go.

Month after month my heart sank with my clockwork like regularity. Due to my "advanced" age, my doctor suggested some testing. My husband and I decided we were not going to venture down that path. If we got pregnant then it was meant to be, if we did not then...

Month after month I began to lose hope. I pushed the issue of intervention one more time, but my husband made it clear that he did not want to go through that. We have, after all, been blessed with three healthy children, and we'd already agreed that we were going to begin the adoption process to open our home to an older child in need of a family. We began to discuss when the optimal time to begin would be. While I still held a glimmer of hope, I began to believe that perhaps the miracle of having a child created from our love would not happen in my womb. I tried to resign myself and started thinking about when I might schedule that surgery.

So there I was in bed, desperate for my husband to wake up. I stared at him and willed his eyes to open. He was snoozing lightly. The sun had already begun to rise and the sky was glorious. He had about 45 minutes until the alarm would sound. I knew he needed his rest. He had also been restless in the night. A good wife would have let him sleep, especially after all the hard work he had put into making my Mother's Day weekend so spectacular. I never said I was a good wife.

I gently rubbed his shoulder. "LOML?" (This is our nickname for each other, it stands for Love Of My Life. I know, I know, newlyweds.) He opened one eye and got his cute morning grin on."Hi LOML." He said."LOML, do you remember the last time I had my period?" I questioned."Umm, I don't think it was that long ago." He said.

I kissed him on his soft sleepy eyelids and let him drift off for the remainder of time before the alarm sent us all scurrying.

The next hour was a blur of missing socks, nothing "good to eat" for breakfast, last-minute forgotten homework assignments attempting to be completed at warp speeds, and my saintly husband agreeing to take the kids into the city for school so I could get more work done by staying behind to work from my home office.

As the garage door made its final clunk on the cement I began doing the math again. My husband was certain I'd had my period recently. I opened my calendar and went day by day, trying to remember the buildings I had been in, people I had met with, and all the places I'd gone to the bathroom. I can barely remember my kid's names, so I was digging pretty deep for memories here. I simply had no recollection.

I put my coffee pod in the Kuerig and went to the fridge to grab the milk. There on the counter was the milk carton. Empty. I decided to run to the store. During the drive, I debated getting a pregnancy test. What was the worst that could happen, I'd waste 12 bucks and my period would start? I was really scared...what if it said I was pregnant? Then what?

I began to imagine the response from my family...my friends... I realized that just two weeks before I had once again seen a 3 in the second position on the scale. It had taken me almost 7 months to get it there. What would happen to my body? What if...what if at 40 I could not manage to "keep" the pregnancy? Fears began to flood my mind and I tried desperately to quell them.

As I entered the store I went directly to the family planning section and struggled with which test to buy. Do I buy the super expensive one to be absolutely sure the results are accurate, or do I believe the store brand that advertises 98% accuracy? And what of that 2%? I decided to split the difference and go for the name brand package that was on sale.

I hoped no one would see me as I slinked to the milk aisle a thousand miles away in the back of the store. I then tried to slip unseen to the self-check lanes. I scanned the bright pink box and a big message pops up on the screen: 'Assistance has been requested. Please remove magnetic tracking device from box.' I flushed with embarrassment. The woman looked over at me, pushed some button on her remote device and said, "You're fine honey." All I could think was, you don't know if I'm fine. I might be pregnant here.

My thoughts tortured me on the seemingly endless 1.5-mile drive home. I walked in the house, put the dog outside for 'privacy', and wondered if I'd be able to pee. Then I remembered my age and the fact that I always have to pee. I opened the package and read the directions carefully, even though I knew them intimately from my pregnancy attempts well over a decade before with my first child. I managed to do what needed to be done and gently placed the test wand on the square of toilet paper I had laid out in advance. Memories of watching the clock and praying for that second line to appear filled my mind. I set the timer on my phone for three minutes and looked over at the wand. In those few moments, two lines had appeared on the screen.

I gasped. I cried. I did not know what to do. Do I call my husband or wait until he comes home? Do I jump in the car and drive the 40 minutes to his office and run in like Rocky, waving the wand in the air? I sat at the kitchen table in shock. Trying to take it all in. Trying to understand what it all meant. Imagining my children's faces, their questions. Fearing my husband's response. Had he relaxed feeling he'd dodged a bullet?

I looked towards my backyard and noticed the leaves beginning to bud on our Aspen trees. The trees were young and sickly looking. We'd feared that the drought had taken its toll on the trees and we had discussed the day before how we might re-plant that area. I grabbed my phone and took a picture of the leaves.

I called my husband."Hello LOML." He answered.Trying to control the quiver in my voice I replied, "Hi baby, guess what?"""What?"" The Aspen's have begun to bloom.""Yay!""Guess what else?"He hesitated. "What else baby?"I began to sob. "I'm pregnant."

I don't remember what else he said. I only remember sobbing, asking if he was happy, telling him I did not know what to do. He sounded happy. He suggested I call my doctor. I thought that was a good idea. I hung up the phone with him and called my OB. I was sure she'd want to see me right away due to my advanced age but no such luck! At 8 weeks along, based on my best guess of the first day of my last period, my appointment was set. It was then that I hit the Internet in search of everything I could find on being pregnant at 40. All of this to say there was not much to be found.

My tradition has been to wait until I am 3 months along and safely in to my second trimester before letting people know about my pregnancy. This time around, we are going to do things differently. Today, after having just returned from a very successful and very exciting first visit with my OB I will begin sharing about my pregnancy in the hopes that I can provide information that is valuable and relevant for other women in their 40's experiencing pregnancy. I invite you to share your own experiences to help others along the journey. With any luck, I'll get the hubster to chime in with what it is like to be going through this all over again when your first child has just graduated from high school.

Wow, have I mentioned I'm pregnant?

Saturday, June 15, 2013

Honoring the Dad about to start all over again

Today I joined the myriad other last minute shoppers, seeking just the right card to celebrate the Dads in our lives. I really wanted to be prepared this year for so many reasons. First, the little ones will understandably be with their biological father this weekend. Some advance work on my end would have ensured that they could have picked out or made cards of their own for their stepfather. Second, I know the teenager won't figure it out on his own and again, a little advance work on my end could have made certain that his dad was not left without any recognition from him another year in a row. Third is the matter of the little peanut roasting inside me. Certainly, my husband deserves a card from the peanut. I'm going to blame this one on the peanut.

Rounding the half way mark of 10 weeks pregnant, I'm still suffering from extreme pregnancy exhaustion. I can barely get the work I need to get done accomplished. The mere thought of any extra time away from the sanctuary of my pillowtop king sized bed directly under the ceiling fan at full steam is simply torture. And by work, I mean stuff I get paid to do. The house is a mess, the laundry unfolded and I have not prepared a meal in over a month.

To further highlight the wackiness of this all, we are talking about some shopping. I needed to hit a store or two, maybe take the kids to the card aisle at the grocery store. I love to shop. Not a little, a lot. Yet, the mere thought of trying to trudge through the mall - or worse, stand in the card aisle while the kids read every single card until they found the funniest one representative of their relationship with this wonderful man - was unbearable. Doesn't everyone know I'm tired?

So, I didn't go. I didn't take the kids. I didn't take the teenager. As I lay in bed next to this man and reflect on what an amazing father he has been, I can barely live with myself. Let's add the whole choreographed Mother's Day weekend he just crafted and executed for me and I can barely stand myself.

When Michael first entered our lives as my boyfriend I invited him to dinner at my town home. The kids were just 6 and 7. He walked through the door, and my little guy walked right up to him and punched him in the stomach with as much energy as his 25lb body could muster. Michael's response? "Hi there, I'm Michael. I know you don't know me yet, but I'd like to know you." I'm paraphrasing a bit. I mean, we are talking about 5 years ago, and I can barely remember this morning. What I remember was the sensitivity. He did not get angry at my son for punching him. He understood that this was challenging. He understood that they would need time to get to know him and trust him.

In no time at all they were climbing all over him and telling him they loved him. No more punches.

I have watched him over the years manage what has been at times an excruciating path to manhood for his son. His son Ryan did not warm up to me as quickly as the little ones warmed up to Michael. He was also twelve when I became a regular part of his life. He had no interest in my involvement in what he considered a men-only relationship between himself and his father. I was in the way.One evening after a considerable post-dinner yelling match where he hurled every insult and curse word he could think of at me he ran out of the house, no shoes on his feet and disappeared into the dark cold night.

The kids and I sat speechless at the table and Michael, after realizing that his son was not coming back through the door, went out into the night to find him. It was maybe an hour later that my son came to me and said, "Ryan is at the back door and crying but says he won't come in." I handed my daughter the phone and told her to call Michael and let him know.

As I approached the door, Ryan began apologizing to me for his behavior towards me and telling me he'd understand if I did not wish for him to come back inside the house again. At about that time his Dad came through the back gate. His son was shaking and crying, and Michael took him in his arms. He had heard the apology. He listened for another hour as his son told him everything that was bothering him. As we would experience several more times over the years as he made his way through middle and high school, I was not the problem. It was a peer or a girl, but I was an easy target for him. I watched as Michael listened and comforted him before grounding him for his treatment of me and of the family. The way Michael handled it all was clearly from a place of love. I had never seen anyone handle a situation so thoroughly and respectfully.

This love, respect, and overall calmness has been a theme in Michael's parenting. That is not to say that he never loses his temper (he is human after all), but it is a rarity. Our children have not been easy. It is never easy when you are blending families. Children come with open wounds and so do parents. I remember once my husband posted a picture on my Facebook wall of a penguin carrying a suitcase. The caption read: the right partner will unpack your baggage with you. We've been unpacking baggage together for several years now and it seems like there is never an end to the next suitcase showing up in our lives.

As the peanut continues to grow inside of me I feel so fortunate that Michael is the father as I know together we will be able to work side by side and help this one through the very difficult work of growing up.

So, you see, not recognizing this man on Father's Day is just plain unconscionable. Today at about 2:30 in the afternoon I finally felt good enough to get out of bed. I made some excuse about a return I had to make and left my husband and the teen to their work building and hanging walls in the basement he has been refinishing.

The mall was torture. I felt like I was swimming through a swamp. I was sweating, thanks to the doubled blood volume in my pregnant body, and I was in a sleepy fog. I made my way through the men's department and found an outfit I think he will love (but would never buy for himself because it is not "work" clothes). After I went to the card shop. I bought a card from the dog and a card from the kids. Then I saw the dad-to-be cards. Each of the cards written for a man about to become a father for the first time. There are no cards for the man who has already raised one child to the brink of manhood who is about to start over again. What would they say? Perhaps: "To the man who was almost about to regain some sanity, what were you thinking???" Maybe it is better that they don't sell any cards for our situation.

So to you, my husband, father of our combined children, father of the little peanut in the womb, I simply say thank you. Thank you for teaching me how to be patient, how to listen more deeply than the angry words being spewed. Thank you for teaching me how to help the little ones through pain, how to love deeply, honestly and with your whole self. Thank you for helping us unpack our baggage and put it away. Thank you for being a special part of our lives. Happy Father's Day.

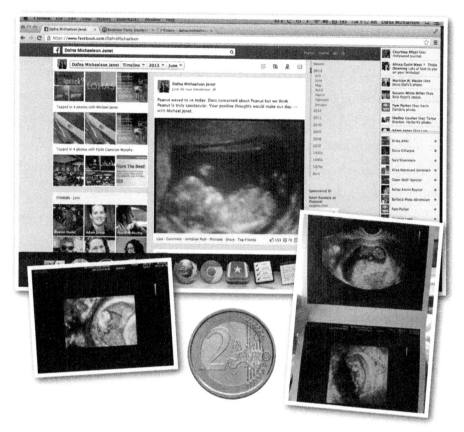

Fear

Pregnancy, testing, chromosomes, and parents' fear

TUESDAY, JULY 2, 2013

To me, there is almost nothing that compares to the excitement that precedes an ultrasound. Each day the baby grows and changes inside of me and try as my husband may, he can't seem to see the Peanut through my very opaque skin. The window that ultrasound provides - to see the normal, healthy development of head, torso, limbs and that furiously beating heart instantly puts us at ease. We can see that everything is going just fine.

At the "advanced maternal age" of 40, I've been offered all sorts of additional testing because of the statistically increased risk of genetic abnormalities in babies born to women of my age. Today's test was looking for nuchal translucency (NT). Defined as a gathering of fluid at the base of the baby's neck, an increase in the nuchal translucency can indicate a higher risk for a chromosomal abnormality or heart defect.

My husband and I eagerly arrived at the appointment. A chance to see Peanut up on the screen. I prepared for the ultrasound and was surprised to learn that I had now progressed far enough into the pregnancy that the normal wand on the abdomen could be used. No more awkward internal invasion for the chance to see Peanut!

The nurse, a super friendly and talkative young woman, squeezed the warm ultrasound gel onto my abdomen and began gently rubbing the wand over my belly. In no time at all Peanut was on the screen and seemed to be waving at us. I reached for my husband's hand and caught the joy in his eyes as he watched his little progeny on the screen. I love these moments. This foreshadowing of the love our child will see when they look into their father's eyes. I was filled with feelings of blessing.

The nurse was pointing out the heart, face, womb before her tone changed and she became quiet. I'm not sure if I was trying to will her past this quiet concern which was now written all over her face or if I was trying to make her comfortable with whatever outcome she was about to reveal to us. I'm not sure why I do this at all but I have noticed it with my recent "bad news" medical deliveries over the past several years: I go to my happy place and face. My "we can handle this" outward expression, I hope, puts the medical practitioner at ease so I can get out of there and try to understand what I've just been told. I felt that it was time.

"Oh, look at that baby!""Isn't Peanut cute baby?""Look at how Peanut is moving about!"

It was awkward. I couldn't stop. I could see the nurse's chest rise and fall and noticed how she was swallowing deeply as if to suppress a sigh. My husband was quiet too. We all knew something just wasn't right on the screen.

As the nurse wiped my belly of the now cooling gel she said, "There is an increase in fluid. I'm going to send the doctor in so he can talk to you about options." She tried to smile but it wasn't there.

I started to have flashbacks of memories. Times when I'd been given medical news I wasn't prepared for. When my first was born, she had a clear cranial abnormality. Our pediatrician referred us to a doctor who has been classified as the top doctor for craniosynostosis. I'd never heard the word before. We spoke to some of the other parents from our Lamaze group. As doctors that had worked professionally with the doc we were referred to, they warned us, "He sees so many patients that he may not give your daughter a thorough evaluation. You are going to have to work to get him to really look at her." My daughter's father and I went in ready for a battle. I'd bar the door with my ample post-pregnancy body, if I had to, to make sure our little girl had a thorough looking at!

We were in one of the oldest buildings at the now demolished Children's Hospital campus in Denver. I remember standing near the old iron heating unit and looking out the window at the Denver city skyline down the hill. The doctor walked in. He was gruff, we were young and nervous. He barely looks at our daughter - as we were warned might happen - and then says "Yeah, we are going to schedule her for surgery at about 6 months." I was frozen. I was supposed to have to argue for a thorough evaluation. He had barely taken one look at her and, what did he just say?

My husband was looking at me. We waited for the doctor to come in. I remained on the table as the nurse had advised me that the doctor would want to look for himself. The doctor walked in, a thin man who looked tired from perhaps one too many deliveries of bad news. He was accompanied by a student who could not have been a day past 15. He began the ultrasound and soon my Peanut was up on the screen again. I love to see that… He begins measuring and measuring again and one more time for… good measure. He tells us that they look to see an NT of 1.7mm or below and that above 2mm they begin to be concerned. (After doing my research and speaking to my Perinatologist (High-Risk Obstetrician) friend I realize that less than 3.0mm-3.5mm is likely still okay.) He does not tell me what my level is, and though I thought to ask, I also thought that maybe I didn't want to know.

He tells me that at this point we have options. He would suggest a chorionic villus sampling or CVS. This test done by placing a thin catheter or tube through the cervix, in my case, and taking a sample from the placenta would give us lots of information about what could be going on. It would be able to tell us if the baby has Down Syndrome, Turner's Syndrome, Trisomy 18, Trisomy 13 or other more esoteric genetic findings. At this point he estimates that my Peanut has "a 50% chance of a chromosomal abnormality or heart defect." The CVS carries with it a 1:200 risk of miscarriage. The nurse would later explain that those numbers may be skewed in the U.S., where we generally only do CVS when an abnormality is detected and therefore the risk of miscarriage is higher to begin with. I still didn't like those odds.

The other option was a relatively new test on the market. It was certainly new to a mom who last gave birth in what may as well be considered the dark ages of 2002. The Maternity T21 test can look for Downs Syndrome as well as Trisomy 13 and Trisomy 18 and the sex chromosomes; it will tell us if Peanut is a boy or a girl. It is less diagnostic than the CVS but is non-invasive. A simple blood draw is all that is needed. No connection at all to increased miscarriage risk. A "positive" or a "negative result would be 99% accurate. A downside is that results generally take up to 2 weeks as opposed to 2 days for the initial testing with CVS. The doctor offered to leave me and Michael alone to discuss. He told us to take all the time we needed and the nurse popped her head in to let us know that she tentatively put us on the calendar for the CVS for their last available slot of the week.

I don't know why we do this (we being women), but the first thing I did when Michael and I were finally alone was apologize to him. Clearly, my ancient eggs and ancient womb must be at fault. He just held my hands in his much larger, much stronger hands and looked me deep in the eyes. I could see the creases of concern on his forehead and the deep emotional bond we share in his eyes.

"What do you want to do?" He asked.My mind was a thousand layers of blank pages. I knew this conversation. I'd had it before. They thought my daughter was going to have Down Syndrome. I remember clearly discussing with her father that neither of us was interested in an abortion. If there were to be challenges we'd meet them. We would not do invasive testing.I felt like I'd had a dress rehearsal for this moment. I had also left my body and was watching this all transpire from a corner of the room where I had curled into a ball.

My husband was waiting for my response."Well, I can't imagine we'd want an abortion... There is a 50% chance that nothing is wrong... Gavi turned out ok... I'm afraid of the CVS... I don't really want to wait 2 weeks but I'd rather be patient than risk the possibility of miscarriage."I'm not certain I was all that coherent. I didn't "feel" like anything was wrong with Peanut. I sensed no foreboding, no overwrought worrying... Floating around and waving at us, my gut was telling me that Peanut was doing fine. I really wanted to believe my gut.

I looked at Michael and said, "This baby is as much yours as mine. What do you think we should do?" I could see his ticker-tape going. We always joke that he has a ticker-tape that runs around his forehead that lets me know what he is thinking. Today was no different. I could see he was worried. I could see that he would not want to push me into anything I did not want to do. I could see that his only concern was bringing Peanut into this world. I guess I was hoping he'd give a definitive answer in the form of a directive. I wanted him to make the decision so I didn't have to. Mature, eh? But that is not my husband's style. He asked me questions. "What will we do with the information when we have it?" "Would you want to terminate?" "If you don't plan on terminating, what difference does it make if we wait 2 weeks or 2 days?" "Will you be able to handle the waiting?" They were all good questions, but I felt there must be right and wrong answers and I forgot to study for the test.

I didn't want to terminate. Neither did he.I wanted to be able to be patient. So did he.

When the doctor returned, we told him we'd opt for the non-invasive blood test. Somehow I felt like I was letting him down. He did not indicate that at all; it was an internal feeling. Any time I've made a decision that differs from my doctor's opinion I worry about what they think of me. I'm working in therapy to resolve this.He was so kind. He tried to make small talk. Asked me about my career. I put on my happy face and tried to have a normal conversation with this giant elephant and an extremely uncomfortable student standing in the middle of the room. He set me up for the blood work and set me up for a follow-up. He shook my hand and told me to call at any time with any concerns or questions. "Don't sit at home worrying. Call anytime." It's 2 AM as I type this. I'm pretty sure he did not mean now.

On the carride home I called my mom. I debated not telling her, but I wanted her support. I knew she'd worry. That's what she does. I wanted her to feel comfortable - as I always want people to feel. I played up my lack of concern. "Remember," I told her, "how they were worried about

Gavi? Can you imagine this world without her??" I told her I was sure it would be alright.

Next, I called my best friend. She was concerned. I could hear her beautiful girls in the background as she tried to get them ready to leave the house for piano lessons. I asked if it was a bad time to talk. She and I have been through it all together. The happiest moments. The scariest moments. The life and death moments. "I'll stay with you on the phone as long as you need." She said. At that moment my phone beeped. It was the OB's office. I knew the antepartum unit had called them. I assumed they were just calling to let me know they were up to speed on the situation. I took the call.

The Doc on the other end was not my regular OB. She wanted, as I'd surmised, to let me know they were aware and that while my Doc was out until next week she was there to answer any of my questions. I told her we'd opted for the blood test. She hesitated. I hate when doctors hesitate. She said, "You know, it's very rare that we see a nuchal translucency this high." I was kicking myself for not asking the first Doc for that number. I sucked it up and asked her what my number was. "Well, usually we are ok with anything under 2. At 3 we worry about heart defects. You were at 4.8." My heart crept into my throat. It sounded so much worse all of a sudden. She continued. "It's just that you have a small window for the CVS testing. It has to be done by 13 weeks."

It's that moment where you know the Doc can't tell you what to do, but she's telling you what to do.

I hung up, called my friend back and just started to sob. Now it felt real. Now I had to crawl out of the corner of the hospital room and be present. Now I had to have another conversation with my husband. We both pulled into the driveway at the same time. I waited for him to gather his things and walk towards me. He could see on my face that something had changed. I cried when I told him about the call. My stomach began to cramp and I looked for a place to sit down.

He kneeled next to me and held me. "You know, this does not really change anything. We still have the same 50% chance. We still have a 50% chance that Peanut will be just fine." He said if I had changed my mind I should call and take the slot for the CVS. Whatever I chose he'd support 100%. I calmed down and decided to stay the course.

Now, we wait. 2 weeks. An eternity and the blink of an eye. We'll make more decisions when we have more information. Meanwhile, we are hanging on the positives. There is a 50% chance that I am carrying a healthy baby that could grow up to be President of the United States. Go Peanut! We love you.

I asked my friend physician and Perinatologist Richard Broth MD for his perspective:

One of the hardest things to do in the field of medicine is to convey information to patients. Some patients want the direct approach while others want the doctor to ease into the results – regardless of what those results are. In the case of pregnancy, in my humble opinion, it is even harder since the parents' expectations are that their child is 100% healthy without any problems or concerns. No one wants or expects to be the one to be told that her child has something going on. However, the reality is that there are many women/couples who are given results like the one that Dafna was given on a daily basis. Most patients aren't as open or eloquent as Dafna, and therefore one wouldn't know this information about them unless she was a close confidant.

As a Perinatologist (specialist in Maternal-Fetal Medicine or High-Risk OB) I have this conversation many times a day/week/month/year. As a general rule, my approach is to be very direct and put the information out to the couple (remove the "elephant" from the room) and then address the issue and the response.

What patients need to understand is that genetic results should not be classified as "good" or "bad". True, no one requests a child with a genetic or physical anomaly, but when that situation occurs it is still the child of those parents, their flesh and blood, and nothing changes that. The result of the ultrasound or laboratory study is a fact and a reality, not a punishment. Many ultimately choose to accept the results and advocate for their child trying to maximize that child's potential (or just providing comfort care until the ultimate outcome occurs). Others may choose to pursue other options. My role, and the role of my staff, is to be there to provide objective counsel and support for any decision that the couple makes, without judgment or prejudice. Everyone makes decisions that best suit her own situation and beliefs, and it is not for me (or anyone for that matter) to judge.

Loss

Saying goodbye to the baby never born

THURSDAY, JULY 25, 2013

I don't want to write this article. I don't want to keep waking up and remembering. I don't want to turn off Netflix and think. I don't like the moments of silence because I soon fill them with tears. I don't want to be sad. I don't want to wallow in misery or self-pity. I don't want to think about all the what-ifs. I want to stop feeling like I am being punished when I know in my heart I was more likely given a gift. I don't want to keep looking at my husband's beautiful eyes and see them tinged with grief. I don't want to feel the emptiness in my womb. I don't want to see the blood in the toilet. I don't want to remember the moment I knew he was gone.

But the happy memories bring me tears.

From the moment I realized I had missed my period to the two pink stripes peering back at me from the pregnancy test, I was in love and I was in fear. I knew my risks. The factor of my age. I knew how deeply I wanted this child conceived in the greatest love. I was determined to do everything within my power to give this child every opportunity for a healthy fetal development. But from the first moment, I knew it was out of my hands. Who this child would be, how this pregnancy would go, boy or girl...all determined before I even knew I was pregnant.

That first ultrasound at 8 weeks. My husband by my side. We cried when we saw the heartbeat. We laughed, we cried, we laughed some more. We couldn't believe the timing: our baby was due the day before my daughter's scheduled Bat Mitzvah. It all just added to the humor of a family sending one child off to Marine Boot Camp as we prepared to welcome another to our world.

Telling the children was the most fun of all. Our daughter had been begging us to give her a baby, sister preferably, from the moment we got married. We planned and colluded to find just the right moment to bring the kids together, over ice cream, of course, to break the news. They were shocked and amazed. They thought we were pulling a prank, but when the reality set in the full range of emotions swept through the kids. We showed them the picture of the first ultrasound and began referring to the baby as Peanut.

The kids rubbed my still flat(ish) tummy and wished Peanut good morning and good night. My daughter got her Red Cross first aid and CPR training and felt ready to care for the child day and night. My son worried about how to be a good role model when he struggles so himself. The Marine Recruit worried that his sibling would not know him, and we planned skype calls and the like. Every conversation had a little bit of extra Peanut joy.

I could not stop talking about it. Every person I met learned that I was pregnant. I am sure it may have been annoying to some, but I could not have been more excited and I had to share. I was also exhausted and VERY nauseous at the beginning and I just felt people needed to know why I was not 100%.

I finally started showing and my husband took me shopping for maternity clothes. "Fat, or pregnant?" was my go to question. Amazing how he never once answered fat. He'd answer "pregnant" with a glow on his face and rub my tummy.

Each morning I'd flip through my ten pregnancy apps and read the daily report. Weekly I'd read it aloud in bed to Michael. It was the weekly Peanut report. We followed his growth from sesame seed to kidney bean, to lime, to apple...

I'd had spotting in the beginning, so when I started spotting at 14 weeks I hoped it was nothing. But in my heart I knew. On the 3rd day of spotting, I called my doc and scheduled an appointment. By the time of the appointment, the spotting had progressed from brown to red. As I drove into the doctor's office I imagined myself saying goodbye to Peanut.

I picked up Michael and together we went into the ultrasound room. She prepped me and there on the screen was our little Peanut. "Okay Peanut, let's see that heartbeat," I remember saying. "Oh honey," the tech said, "There's the heart, and it is not beating anymore. I'm so sorry."

My mind went blank. I kept looking at the image on the screen, willing that heart to beat, but I had known that Peanut was gone. I just didn't want to admit it to myself.

The team at my doctor's office was great. They hugged me. They brought me water. They comforted me. Michael held me in his arms and we cried and sobbed. Mere minutes before we were sitting in the waiting room figuring out where to go for lunch. In a moment it seemed our world had come crashing down around us.

Continuing my thoughts from yesterday...

I wake up in the morning and there is this twilight moment where I can't figure out what is missing. And then I remember. It happens each morning, this depth of emptiness I have never known. I've know loss. I've known deep loss. When my grandmother passed 2.5 years ago, I thought I would never recover from the void. She was so important to my world. Her love filled me in so many ways. I knew her, I felt her physically, she held me from my tiniest days through adulthood. I never got to hold Peanut in my arms and they ache for that. I ache for the feeling of him in my womb. I ache for my belly, just a few days ago hard with a baby but now mushy from over-indulgences in ice cream and pasta. It is all I wanted to eat while pregnant.

I bought a stuffie for Peanut on my recent trip to Oregon. My friend Linda stopped by a wonderful little floral and gift shop on the way from the airport to my hotel. There in the back was the cutest little red stuffed rhino/dino. He was so soft and so sweet looking. It would be Peanut's first friend. We named him Stewart. I sleep with Stewart each night and wake with him near my belly as though he is looking for Peanut. His little red face looks so sad to me now.

As my days go on and the baby bump that was forming continues to disappear, I can't believe that just a week ago I was pregnant and now nothing to show but some weight gain. And I had worked so hard to lose the weight I had packed on after last year's hip surgery. I have no energy for dieting again.

I apologize for the randomness of my thoughts. I can't yet keep a consistent stream. I really try not to because when I do I end up here, it ends in tears and hurt and pain. I don't like to be in this place.

I fill my day with distractions. I watched all 13 episodes of Orange is the New Black in 2 days. (Great show BTW.) I'm trying to get into Arrested Development, but the story line is too shallow to keep my mind preoccupied. I weeded the whole lawn, a task I had not been able to complete while pregnant. It was hard. The weeds were taking over. I worked up a serious sweat. I weeded until I felt like I would pass out, and then I picked up where I left off a few hours later. And yet it hurt me to weed. I can't explain the thought process, but while I wanted to annihilate the weeds, I didn't want to take away any more life in this world. I know rationally that I did not take away Peanut's life, but he died in my womb. In my womb. Inside my body where I so desperately believed I could keep him safe. It is outside the womb that my children face risks every day. Inside my womb was where I was so careful about everything that entered my body. They are supposed to be safe from harm in there.

Today Michael had to go into the office for his board meeting. He did not want to go. He did not want to leave me. I did not want him to go, but I understood that he had no choice. I also believe that we have to get back to living life. I am alone for the first time since that moment we learned that Peanut's little heartbeat was no more. I am scared. I don't like being alone with my thoughts. When Michael is here I feel a responsibility to move forward, to smile, to distract him. We spent hours looking online at cruises we simply have no money to take. But it felt good to dream of ocean air, of dressing up for dinner, of dancing, of making love. Now alone in the house I am haunted. I have little pictures of our ultrasounds of Peanut everywhere. Not in frames, but just laying on the counter where the family could enjoy them. A window into our new family member.

I know I must move forward. My little guy is struggling and will be home soon. His anxiety will peak when he learns that Peanut is no more. My daughter will be home a few weeks later. She too will be devastated at the loss of her sibling she ached for, begged for and dreamed of. Our Marine Recruit is in the midst of boot camp, so he won't know until October. We don't want to distract him from the grueling work physical and mental work that he must do in his daily march towards his own dreams and the making of his own adult life. We won't be able to mourn as a family for some time.

I have moments of normalcy. I canceled my engagements this week. I am not ready to face the world. In truth, I am afraid to speak to people. I can't handle speaking aloud the words that run through my mind to this page. I had to go over the details for a session I was to lead in Rifle, Colorado tomorrow. I was so looking forward to working with this group. This is a group of individuals working to revive Main Street in many small towns around our state. When I traveled to all 50 states, some of the most amazing community builders I met were working around the revivals of their own Main Street. There is much promise in this type of development and I was so thrilled to even be asked. I sat on the phone with my friend Darcy, going point by point over the agenda: Define community, create a social media mission statement, Build consensus, Understand the unique language of platforms, Learn to engage... I was alive. I love my work. I live to present. 3 opportunities to connect, engage and empower community builders and small business leaders lost. I was so looking forward to this week. I loved standing in front of rooms of people who came to hear me speak dressed in my pretty maternity dresses my baby bump proudly on display. Laughing with the group when I stumbled and blaming pregnancy brain...now I have to go back to blaming my age, they say the memory is the second thing to go... Next week I will be back on the road. I have to prepare to face my new "normal."

How do we do it? To my mother's discomfort, I am very open on Facebook. I write about parenting in that I hope others will relate, pick up a helpful tool, laugh and so I share. I shared about this pregnancy early on. I heard immediately from a slew of incredible, smart, powerful women who all had babies in their 40's. I know a number of their exceptional progeny. I enjoyed sharing about dealing with 40 and dealing with pregnancy. You were all there for us when we got the first hint of trouble. You all celebrated with us when we received the first step of promising news. Those who knew were holding your breath with us while we waited for the heart scan which was scheduled for next week. You share your stories with us. You made us laugh. You made us cry. You made us pray. When I posted our painful news you were there for us again. Though I have not responded I have read every single message. I have ached for how many of you have losses of your own. I hold promise as I see that you who have lost have moved from pain to being able to see and share the joy. I am comforted by your words of friendship.

My joy will be around the moments of absolute wonder Peanut brought us. There were so many over the short 4 months of his existence. It was that last ultrasound where he waved at the screen. We now know that only a few days later his heart stopped. He was waving goodbye.

Daddy and I love you so much Peanut. You will always be a part of our family, even though we never got to hold you, we never got to kiss you, your sister and her friends never got to make you their dress up toy. I miss you so deeply that the breath leaves my lungs when I think about you. I will fill that emptiness with your tiny soul and it will bring me joy. What fun you were coming so unexpectedly, trying to share your grand entrance with your sister's bat mitzvah celebration. And you left at the time you were supposed to leaving us to wonder but know in our hearts that your purpose was served here. I know that these words are hollow right now but they are the basis for my healing. I love you Peanut. I will always love you Peanut. Thank you for being a part of me for even a brief blip on the screen. You are my child and I hold you in my heart next to your brothers and sister. This morning Daddy's friend wrote to say that her little girl was out there waiting to play with you. She surmises that the two of you are probably already the best of friends. So many of my friends

A Father's loss

Wednesday, July 24, 2013

SHATTERED: BY MICHAEL JENET

We all have different Journeys to live.

None of us knows how long or how short our Journey will be. For some of us, we will be fortunate enough to live long full lives. For others, those lives are cut short. Always too short.

My wife Dafna and I found out she was pregnant the day after Mother's Day. We both have children from previous marriages. This was our first together. We had been trying and actually had silently given up hope that it would happen. But it did.

We were thrilled. We're both in our 40's, she nearing 41, I at 46. The doctors warned us of all the statistics but said everything looked good.

She had morning sickness. She was exhausted the first few months. This wasn't like being pregnant in your twenties. Still, we were thrilled.

We waited until we had reached the eight-week mark to visit the doctor. We went for the first visit, we had the first ultrasound.

My wife and I held our collective breaths as the technician prepared the machine and then suddenly there was a picture. Our little 'Peanut' on the screen.

It was amazing. My heart jumped, my wife reached out with her hand and we both virtually jumped with joy.

We met with the doctor. She was great and knew how we had been trying. Herself newly pregnant, she was excited for us.

We talked about testing. The usual amnio tests, and also a new one. It had only been out 18 months and was done via blood and ultrasound. It tested for

Downs Syndrome and Trisomy 13 and Trisomy 18, three of the biggest chromosomal challenges 'older' parents have to worry about.

We liked the idea that it wasn't invasive, just a blood test. We agreed to schedule an appointment around 11-12 weeks to have the new test done rather than the traditional invasive ones. There was an added benefit; we could find out if Peanut was a boy or girl.

We couldn't wait to tell our children.

Our daughter was convinced it was a girl. We started talking about names for a girl. The whole family (daughter, two sons) chimed in with ideas.

Then we shared it with the world on Facebook.

Our friends were overjoyed. Our hearts leaped.

We went in for the new test just after our 11-week mark.

The technician was nice, she started the ultrasound and once again my heart burst with joy as Peanut came up on the screen, but there was a noticeable change in the technician's demeanor when she saw the screen. She was quieter, moving the wand around, clicking keys.

When she finished, she told us there was more fluid behind Peanut's neck than they liked.

A doctor came in next and explained that we had a 50-50 chance that something was wrong.

They took the blood.

It would take 8-10 days for results and we had the 4th of July coming up which would extend the time.

We waited. I was worried, scared, hopeful, scared, and well... scared.

Dafna was confident. She didn't feel like anything was wrong. I fed off her enthusiasm. Peanut was strong. He was going to be alright.

The days stretched, hour by hour. We waited with bated breath.

On July 8th, the Dr's. Office called with the news that the test results came back ok. No Downs, no Trisomy 13 or 18.

My heart soared. We were so happy. Now moving into the second Trimester we knew the odds were getting better. We also now knew that Peanut was a boy. Our daughter was disappointed but still happy about the baby. We started talking about possible boy names wanting to find a way to honor my Father and somehow incorporate my wife's Grandmother.

We went to Baby's-R-Us just to look around, talking about strollers and cribs, bouncy seats and car seats, clothes, food. We were like young twenty-year old's not seasoned parents. We didn't care. We are so in love and the thought of having a baby together was a miracle and we wanted to enjoy every minute of it.

We had pictures from the ultrasounds, in one Peanut had his arm up waving.

We looked at them repeatedly.

We talked about colors for the baby's room and even talked about painting a mural.

As we approached week 15 my wife started feeling different. She wanted to see another 'picture' of Peanut and our next appointment wasn't due for two more weeks.

She started spotting. It was brown, not red and we knew that could just be normal.

You know how this is going to end.

Two days in a row, then the blood was red. Still spotting but red.

We called for an appointment. The weekend was here, we'd have to wait till Monday.

She continued to spot, though brown again.

I wasn't worried. Peanut was strong. Hope.

My wife thought she could feel a kick, though it was probably too early.

She was worried, I could tell. Everything will be fine I kept telling her. I hoped.

We got to the office, and they started the ultrasound.

There he was, up on the screen. My heart leapt again. See, I thought, there he is, Peanut is right there, everything's fine.

But my wife knew better. Her first words were, 'Now let's see his heartbeat'

Heartbeat? Of course we'll see his heartbeat, I thought. I could see his beautiful little body on the screen, of course we'd hear his heart beat any second now.

And then the technician said the three words that changed everything.

"I'm so sorry"

I could use any number of words to describe what happened next. I was desolate, heartbroken, shocked, crushed... pick one.

The only one that comes close is one that describes what happened to my heart.

It Shattered.

It shattered into a million fragments. Like a floor to ceiling picture window looking out onto a breathtaking vista with blue skies and wispy clouds when suddenly someone slams a large boulder into it and pieces go flying in every direction.

I stared at the screen, unable to breathe.

My heart was breaking, pieces seeming to leave my body and fall onto the floor in front of me while at the same time a huge weight seemed to be crushing it from the inside.

My wife held out her hand, tears falling down her cheeks as I reached out with my own hand. I couldn't stop staring at the screen.

How could this be?

Peanut was right there. I could see him.

The technician pointed out his hands and feet as she measured him.

His tiny, strong, beautiful little heart had stopped beating sometime after the 13th week.

The technician left the room.

My wife and I held each other and cried. No silent tears; hard, deep, sobbing, Pain.

The technician gave us a hug as she moved us into another room to wait to talk to our doctor. We cried some more. A nurse came in and gave us a hug and told us how sorry they were. The whole staff was great.

We simply cried.

All the joy of Peanut was suddenly replaced with a loss so deep, so raw, so filled with pain we couldn't see past the tears. Our world became a blur through tears of anguish far more wracking than anything we had ever known before.

I can't remember the conversation with the Doctor. She was and is wonderful, but I couldn't hear her.

In the minutes that passed while we waited for her my wife and I held each other, repeated that we loved each other. We stared out the window and then without warning sobbed in each other's arms.

I tried to get my head to wrap itself around this new reality. A world without our little Peanut in it.

One moment I was staring out the window trying to understand the impossible, the next my heart, which had already exploded seemed to somehow shatter again, into even smaller pieces, and tears streamed down my face as I tried to find a way to breathe.

I held my wife, close, tight. Telling her over and over again how much I loved her as if somehow that would help the anguish I knew all too well she was feeling.

Somehow, we made it home. We had to call another doctor and schedule a D&C.

I couldn't imagine how my wife was feeling.

I had been so happy and full of joy seeing Peanut's little image from the ultrasounds, but she had felt him growing inside of her. She had seen her body change, felt the physical changes inside her and rubbed her tummy knowing inside of her a tiny little life was growing.

And now, Peanut was growing no more.

She was beyond desolate. Inconsolably sad and now she had to have a procedure to remove Peanut from her. I knew she was struggling with the idea that he was no longer growing inside of her, his heart no longer beating and yet the idea of his leaving her physically was one more cruel step in an already brutal reality.

I put her to bed so she could rest and wandered through our home, a usually happy and serene calming house we've made our own, and now I wandered through it in despondent silence. I tried to watch a movie, anything to take my mind off the hell of the life I was living.

One minute I was seemingly fine. The next I was sobbing uncontrollably on the floor.

I went upstairs to check on my wife, she was sobbing and it happened again. My heart shattering all over again like some cruel and twisted version of the movie Groundhog Day where I had to re-live the pieces breaking repeatedly.

This time, it wasn't simply shattering over the loss of Peanut, though certainly that. This time it was breaking and re-breaking and breaking all over again at the pain my beautiful amazing wonderful wife was suffering through.

I held her, I cried with her, I tried to comfort her and more than anything I wanted to take away the pain for her. To somehow make her feel whole again. To fill the void she was aching from.

I would have done anything, given anything to keep her from the pain that was wracking her mind, body, and soul.

Exhausted we went to bed. Each with our own nightmares only to wake up and realize they weren't nightmares at all but the reality of our new day, our new lives.

We cried and cried, holding each other, offering words of comfort, professions of love, and profound sadness at the loss of our little Peanut.

It's only the second day since we found out Peanut was no longer with us. We have to go to another Doctor for the D&C.

They're very nice. We're both scared.

They normally don't let men go back when they call your name. I'm not sure I would have been polite if they hadn't made an exception. They let me go back and stay with Dafna while they prepped her. IV lines, lots of questions, the nice Doctor letting us know this is a simple medical procedure and that everything will be fine.

He looks me in the eye and with a gentle but firm voice tells me that everything will be ok.

It's not okay, but I know what he means.

I'm ushered into the waiting room. Alone, just as my wife is now alone for the first time since we learned of Peanut's heart stopping. Each of us is alone with our thoughts, only she's about to have a 'procedure'. I ache for her. I want to hold her, to tell her I love her and that everything will be alright, but I can't. Even if I could I wouldn't be able to see her through the stream of tears.

A nurse comes out after about 10 minutes to tell me that everything is fine and asks if we wanted some genetic testing done on the baby. "What does that involve?" I ask her. "About $1,000," she says.

That's not what I was asking. "No," I say, "What would happen? Are you talking about an autopsy?"

"Yes," she says

I tell her no. Dafna and I talked briefly about that on the ride to the office and the one thing she had said was she didn't want something like that happening to Peanut. I agreed.

I sat in the waiting from for another 40 minutes.

Left alone to your own devices, your mind starts to lose any ability to reason. Why hadn't they come back to take me to my wife? They said everything had gone well, surely she would be in the recovery room by now.

I started to panic. Had something gone wrong? Was my wife in trouble and people were frantically trying to help her and I just didn't know? I looked at the people at the reception desk trying to gauge if there was an emergency going on somewhere in the office. At one point an administrator walked by and looked straight at me with a hard stare as she passed. My heart started shattering all over again.

I couldn't lose Peanut and my wife. I couldn't take that. I was panicked, frightened, unable to speak or move. My heart was shattering, again.

A patient who had heard us check in and overheard us telling the reception nurse that our baby's heart had stopped beating two weeks ago came out of the door into the office. As she walked by

towards the exit door, right next to the chair I was sitting in, she opened the door and took a step out, then paused. She leaned back in and turned her head towards me.

"I'm sorry," she said, and then she left.

Two words. Simple. Heartfelt. Caring.

I broke down crying. People stared. I didn't care.

I cried for Peanut. I cried for the fear of something bad happening to Dafna. I cried for me.

They finally came and took me to her. She was fine... at least physically.

She cried. I cried. Her first words to me were "No more Peanut".

I held her close. I told her I loved her. She told me she loved me too.

We eventually went home. We cried endless tears.

I know that crying is part of grief. It's how we get it out of us. I feel as though I won't ever be able to stop.

My wife keeps saying she's sorry. As though this is somehow her fault. She asks me if this happened because of something she did, or felt, or said. The next morning, she woke up and said she felt as though she was being punished.

I know none of this is true. Peanut's little heart simply stopped. For reason's we will never know but certainly not because of something my incredibly wonderful wife could have done or not do. I know how loving and kind and wonderful she is and no one loved Peanut more than she.

And yet, I know what she's going through because I too am struggling with guilt. Is it my fault, my genes, my chromosomes at 46 that caused Peanut's heart to stop beating?

Once again, inexplicably, my heart shatters.

How can I help the love of my life through this pain? I can't even help myself.

I feel a little stronger. I know now how lucky I am to have my wife. I was so scared in the waiting room, afraid of losing her, to have her back has made me more grateful than ever. But I still break down in tears of pain over our poor little Peanut.

And then those moments, when her heart pours out through her tears, when her body sobs and shakes from anguish my heart shatters again as I try to comfort her and hold her, loving her and willing my love could somehow help her, knowing that it can't.

Another night. More dreams. Another morning. Day 3 without Peanut.

Only today isn't just Day 3. Life can be a real bitch sometimes.

Today is the 5th Anniversary of my Father's death.

I feel my heart starting to Shatter all over again. I can't take this. It's too much.

I have no choice.

Five years ago, I remember feeling this pain as Cancer took my Dad away. I remember trying to stay strong for my stepmother whose life was being ripped away from her. I remember crying myself to sleep as we made preparations for his funeral. I remember the pain because it's happening to me all over again.

Five years.

I know now that I mostly remember the good things about my Dad.

I miss him, often. But I also think about the good times, the happiness of cooking with him, learning from him, talking to him. I know that although this time of year is never one I relish, that most days I think of him fondly.

And so I know that in time this pain won't erase the joy and happiness Peanut brought to our lives. I know I'll think of him and smile. In time, I'll be able to remember the joy he brought to Dafna and me and the excitement and love we had for him. In time. His Journey was just shorter than ours, but that doesn't mean it was any less impact-full. He was loved and brought love to us. He waved and moved and he moved us. He brought us joy, and happiness, and love. We will always remember him and we will always love him.

Today I can only sit and stare. The same way I stared at the screen when those three dreadful words hit my ears. Staring at the impossible.

I sit and stare at the remnants of my heart, shattered into a million pieces on the floor in front of me. Crying for Peanut. Crying for my wife. Crying for my Dad.

Crying.

And my heart SHATTERS all over again.

Saturday, July 27, 2013

My before smile and my after smile

Sometimes when I can't sleep I flip through the pictures on my phone. I take lots of pictures. Pictures of flowers, pictures of food. Pictures of my husband snoozing. He's so cute... Pictures of my kids. Pictures of me hanging out with friends.

This pre-sunrise morning, being no different than most, my sleeplessness led me to flip through my album. There, about 5 pictures in, was the last picture taken of me before learning that my son had died in my womb.

It had been a great night. My husband and I had spent the evening together live tweeting the second to last Biennial of the Americas round table discussion. The talk had been Reinventing Business as Usual. It had been exhilarating. Not only the content we were sharing via Twitter, the experience of sitting next to my favorite human on the planet, the man who has the devotion of my heart and has set wings to my spirit and working on sharing these powerful tweets while snuggled together in the back of the theater my belly swollen with his child inside of me. You couldn't wipe the smile from my face if you tried. I was on top of the world.

My dear friend was a row in front of us, and we planned to meet another lovely couple for tapas downtown when the tweeting was done.

The three of us traipsing downtown on a Thursday evening like young urbanites living the good life.

Dinner was filled with laughter and good drinks, a virgin Long Island iced tea for me and a house special for the rest of the table. My friend's husband snapped a picture of the three ladies. It is this picture that dwells in the camera roll on my phone. A reminder of before.

My smile is huge. It always has been. But in this picture, in particular, it is ear-to-ear. You can just barely see my baby bump. Well, I can see it. I know it was there. I'm wearing the spectacular maternity dress my husband and I picked out at the Gap just a few weeks earlier. It is a floral, boat neck, a strappy number that we paid $6.40 for after applicable discounts. I love nothing more than a fabulous find for less than the tax I pay on most items. I just loved the compliments, the fit, the bump. On. Top. Of. The. World.

I look at the picture now, 5 days since I knew for sure he was gone, and I don't recognize the woman in the photo. It seems like it must have been taken decades ago in a simpler time. The image reflected back to me is completely devoid of pain. It exudes a vibrancy that I can't imagine. A naïveté.

I love smiles. I am the annoying email crafter with two or three smiles made with colon and parenthesis littering your message. And normally that is *after* I've edited the email to change all the exclamation points to periods and reduce the number of smiley faces. I know it's unprofessional. They come out because I am excited about what I am communicating with you, and I want you to feel my smile on the screen.

I also love to capture that true smile that resides in each of us when I take pictures. I have this great shot that my husband captured of his son during one of our family picture adventures. He's leaning on a wagon wheel, and I got him to laugh at the moment my husband clicked the shutter. It's beautiful. It captures his true essence. It is not the forced smile we have all been taught to pull out for the camera. The point between grimace and gritting of teeth that sometimes fills the screen. This was true. Authentic. The happy essence within clearly filling his maturing face.

That was my smile that evening. It came quickly and easily.

Since that awful moment of seeing my poor baby on screen with no heartbeat, I have not been able to find that smile. I want to smile. I rather enjoy smiling. I like it because it puts others at ease. I've tried watching funny movies, but the laughter is forced and physically painful. It's not that I don't think I should smile, it's just that I don't know if I can ever feel the wholeness of my smile of before.

Time heals all wounds. I've been told. I nod. I crack a grin. It hurts when I do.

I ventured out of the house yesterday. We went for a cup of coffee. The young woman at the register unwittingly greeted me with a huge smile and "Welcome! How are you today!?!" She did not know the depths of our pain. She did not deserve to feel my pain. My mind answered "F!#*!ing Sh*#!tty. My baby died." My mouth, fortunately, said, "Fine. Thank you." I attempted to meet her smile with one of my own. I felt like a fraud.

I don't know how long my smiles will hurt or have to be faked. I consider them to be amongst the most important tools in my toolbox for connecting with people and putting them at ease. It works because my smiles are genuine and felt not only in my face but in my whole body. They are a part of my communication system.

My 11-year-old son came home from camp yesterday. His heart shattered, like my husbands, when he learned his baby brother was no longer. He pulled out a beautiful mobile he crafted from branches, beads and fishing line for his brother. I put on the biggest smile in my arsenal to try to calm him. To let him know that while we are so sad we must go on and we will now honor our little Peanut's memory with his handiwork. I searched his eyes for a reflection of the smile he saw on my face but all I saw in his tear-filled eyes were a reflection of the deep sadness in my heart.

A smile is not only in the upturned corners of your mouth. A smile is the twinkle and sparkle of your eyes. The windows to all unspoken secrets and emotions. Is it possible for the after-smile to hold the twinkle and pull of the before-smile? Does life feel that way again? I hope so. I love my before smile.

We have purchased a tree to plant in memory of our unfulfilled dream. I wrote some words that I'd like to carve on a garden stone. My husband gently looked at me and said, "Those are some sad words, they reflect how we feel right now. I want this to be a happy place." So, we will write happy words about love and kindness and dreams and I will work at finding the 'before' smile. Perhaps I will find it under our Peanut tree.

The end

There has to be a better way

July 29, 2013

I changed. In the moment I noticed that my baby's heart was not beating on the ultrasound screen. When the words, which now play over and over in my head in slow motion, "I'm so sorry, that's the heart and there is no heartbeat" reached my ears, I changed. Part of me died in that moment too.

I lay there in shock. I was confused. I didn't know the script, but I knew that I didn't know my lines. What was going to happen next? What was I supposed to do? I had a dead baby inside of me. I asked my husband, "what do we do?" And while trying to comfort himself and me he also tried to keep me calm. "We'll ask the doctor when she comes in."

We waited for what seemed an eternity. In hindsight, we understand we were close enough to the office closing for lunch and the staff wanted to give us as much time as we needed and dignity to leave without having to pass a waiting room full of healthy pregnant women. When she came in and I asked what comes next, she told me about the clinic they send women to who are in my situation. She gave me the name of the doctor and his number written on a prescription pad. She hugged me and asked to see me two weeks after the procedure.

I don't know what I expected. We were just two hours from learning the news. I called the number. I sobbed to the woman who answered the phone. She suggested I call back later. That put me off a bit but really, I was incoherent. I pulled myself together and said, "No, I need to get this scheduled now." I explained that my baby had died and I needed a D&C. She scheduled me for the next morning.

My head was spinning. I did not know how to behave. I did not know how to feel. I knew I felt awful. I knew I felt robbed. I knew I was still in shock. I also knew that I wanted to bury my baby. I did not know how to do anything. I reached out to my Rabbi and he gave me the name of someone to contact. He was a close friend which made it a little easier. I could not speak on the phone, I truly was not ready to hear the voice of another, in truth I am still not ready, so I sent him a message on Facebook. It was already late at night.

The next morning we went. I began bleeding on the way. We got to the office and I was in a bit of shock.

Now, I beg you to please not politicize the sentiments I am about to share with you. This is not intended to be political nor to reflect my beliefs about any form of medical practice. Please.

We came in and there were two young women behind a glass partition. I told them who I was and they asked for $545. It would not be put on my insurance. I questioned them further. "It's a termination so that is not covered by insurance." I was confused and angry. This was no termination, had they not heard me? "My baby died," I repeated firmly. I could see that my husband was confused and did not know how to protect me or to help and let's not forget, his baby died too. The woman in the back of the room stood up and came to the window. "If you want to use your insurance you have to go to the emergency room. I'm not sure if they will help you though." I was confused, and hurting, and bleeding. Why would she send me away? Why would I go to the emergency room and sit there to be possibly sent home? Why were they being so crass? I knew I did not want to leave. I also did not want to stay. I also did not want my dead baby inside of me for one more minute. I wanted my alive baby back.

As we sat and waited to be called back all I could think about was that I had not arranged a burial and I did not know what to do about that. When they called me back and I asked to have my husband come with me I could tell that I had made an unusual request. This confused me further but by this point, after signing all the paperwork, it finally hit me. This was an abortion clinic. Yes, they also perform D&C for fetal demise as in my case but it is the rare case.

My husband came back and they began to prep me. The room was spartan. The equipment seemed old. I started to have nightmares about rusty needles. I could see that everything was wrapped and clean as it should have been but it truly felt awful.

They pulled out a small ultrasound machine. They were looking at the baby. They kept the screen away from me. I really wanted to see my Peanut one more time but I was too afraid to ask. This becomes a theme for me... When they asked Michael to leave me so they could start the procedure I asked, "What will you do with the baby?" She responded quickly "It will all be incinerated."

My mind went blank and then scared. Incinerated? I did not want my baby incinerated. I wanted my baby buried. Well, I did not want that either, I just wanted my baby to be alive and healthy. Once more I failed myself and Peanut. I said nothing in response.

As I was waking from the procedure I asked the nurse "Was the baby formed?" She said no but I still think she was lying. I asked a second nurse, I think it was a second nurse I was still very foggy "Was the baby formed?" She too said no.

I did not have any strength. They helped me to the recovery chairs. A room of five recliners. Five recliners? I could not imagine having to recover with five other women around me. Fortunately, there were none. I asked for my husband and when he came all I could say was "no more Peanut." Even then I could not ask him to help me find the baby and get him buried.

These past nights I panic thinking of my poor baby in an incinerator and knowing I put him there because I did not have the strength to ask for a burial. I had so few tasks here on earth for Peanut and I could not complete this one most basic and most important of tasks. I could not give him a respectful end. I sent him to the incinerator.

I have nightmares. They happen while I am awake or asleep. They happen when I am alone. I wish I had known what to do, how to handle myself. What to say to get the help and the dignified end to a too short life that I would have wanted. But who wants to be prepared for that? We make birth plans when we are pregnant not the opposite. I will be giving this to my obstetrician, a truly wonderful woman, in the hopes that something can be done to make the process one that provides dignity to the mom, respect to the dad and closure for the spirit of a baby we never got to meet. I want to say rest in peace to my little Peanut but I fear I did not provide him with such an end.

Wednesday, July 31, 2013

RETURNING TO WORK WHILE THE GRIEF OF MISCARRIAGE IS STILL RAW

I woke in the morning with anxiety and a headache. One week to the day from my D&C and I was set to return to work. I had not been working since the Monday before when my husband Michael and I first learned our baby boy had died in my womb. Michael returned to work Monday.

I went with him, not quite ready to not be by his side. Tuesday I was set to leave Denver and head to Seattle to live tweet an event and present to small business owners. I love these trips. I love to travel. I live to present. I don't know what I was thinking would happen as I walked through the doors of Denver International Airport but the usual lift of excitement that generally propels me through the airport was gone. Every step was heavy. The paths towards my gate seemed to elongate before my eyes. Every forward motion of my feet taking me further and further my husband.

These trips are always so much fun for me as the team I work with comes together at our event location from around the country. We work well together and we play well together decompressing after each event with laughter and jaunts to local tourist traps and favorite local food stands. Philly cheesesteak in Philly, the shredded beef joint in Chicago, and yesterday the Ferris wheel in Seattle.

I felt an incredible need to keep the conversation light. Each person who hugged me and said they were sorry. I told them, "It's okay," feeling that it was my responsibility to put them at ease. They asked me how I was. I answered with some honesty. "Pretty crappy..." before adding, "but fine." I did not want any of these wonderful people to be burdened by my overwhelming sadness. I did not want to cast a pall. Quite frankly I also did not want to feel the weight of my own sadness crushing my soul.

I walked through the Pike Place Market, teeming with people, with my sister-like friend and colleague and at each stall I found myself searching for something that would ease my pain. This is not the time for me to spend large amounts of money on the healing stones artfully molded into silver necklaces and rings for hundreds of dollars but I found a small stone with a hand etched in the center a raised heart coming out of the palm. $11. I bought the stone.

As we walked through the market to meet the others for dinner I tightly clasped the stone in my palm, holding on for dear life. With my thumb, I could feel the raised outline of the heart. I rubbed and squeezed pouring my sad energy from every pore of my body into the heat of the stone. The heart was my baby Peanut. If I could no longer feel him in my womb, at least I could rub this little heart and feel as though he was with me.

My greatest grief is the loss of feeling him inside me. In those last days I was sure I could feel him move around and the gentle early sensation of kicking. I know now that I was wrong. He was already gone as I focused so hard and so desperately wanted to feel his movements. I miss rubbing my tummy and feeling that in those moments Peanut was feeling my love and the closeness of being wrapped in me as he grew. I dreamed of those moments after birth when he would be set upon my abdomen and then brought to my chest for a first kiss. I agonized about missing out on breastfeeding, as I had bilateral mastectomies several years ago, so no longer have the equipment to perform the miracle of nurturing my child from my body. I mourned that loss not once imagining that I'd never even get to feel the warmth and weight of my baby in my arms.

I lay here in my hotel bed at 4:00 in the morning listening to the seagulls over the vast Seattle waterfront, and my arms physically ache for the feeling of my baby. They hurt. The muscles were ready for the daily task of lifting baby safely nestled in his car seat into the backseat for our daily adventures. Ready for the dozens of lifts up to the changing table for clean diapers. Ready for the evening ritual of bath time in the infant bath next to the sink. Ready for rocking to sleep while singing evening prayers and for soothing fears and sadness and the angst that sometimes comes along with being a baby.

My arms are empty. They hurt and they ache to know they are to remain empty.

In a few more hours the sun will rise over the glistening waters and the rush of morning traffic will fill the streets. Hundreds of small business owners will fill the rooms we have prepared for our events and I will put on my best smile and greet each of these individuals with the respect they are due for taking risks most of us will never face and being the small unrecognized army that bolsters our economy with each new product they bring to market and each new person they employ. They deserve my respect and full attention. They deserve for me to be on.

I miss my husband beyond words. My uterus cramps and aches. My arms seek the comfort of holding my Peanut. But my body will begin the march forward. I will do my work and I will keep my little rock in the palm of my hand to give me strength and make me feel, even for just a minute, that I am stroking the heart of my Peanut and that he is near.

Thursday, August 1, 2013

THE SEARCH FOR COMFORT

Over the past week since I lost my baby I have had what I would consider a lot of unusual behavior compared to my normal behavior. It does not take a degree in psychology to figure out what I have been doing. I have been on a constant search for comfort.

In the past week, I have watched more television than I usually watch in a year. I have been glued to my husband, in a state of near panic when I must be separated from him for any period of time. I have had more to drink than, again, I generally drink in a year. I have had a constant stream of chocolate and fried or fatty foods. I generally watch my food intake closely because of my predisposition for obesity and diabetes but right now I am constantly hungry and nothing seems to fill me. I bought a necklace with my husband with a mother and child molded out of silver. I bought a stone with a hand and heart carved into it. I now know some call these 'worry stones.' I bought new clothes. (Less unusual for me.) I sought solace in a Catholic church... I'm Jewish.

Eating is my normal coping mechanism. I worry about it because I'd already gained pregnancy weight. While I was pregnant I was less worried because I'd figured out my postpartum diet and exercise plan. I'd already begun checking out jogging stroller reviews with my husband. But now, no pregnancy and no baby, I can't find the motivation I need to not only exercise but to stop the destructive eating cycle.

The drinking doesn't feel good. Not even for the few minutes of rush that you get from that tipsy loose feeling. My grandfather was an alcoholic. A nasty one. I know that alcoholism, like diabetes, can be genetic. I certainly don't need to become an alcoholic at this stage of life. These thoughts fill my head when I have a drink, taking away any momentary relief from a glass of wine and replacing it with concern, guilt, and sadness.

Television, while less destructive to my body, also does little to quell the internal angst of loss. I lay there half paying attention to the show while absentmindedly rubbing my now empty tummy and mourning my loss. I can't concentrate on the story lines and I also begin to bemoan my laziness and the lethargy that follows.

Shopping does not even give me the momentary high of finding a good deal and celebrating a new purchase. I feel remorse before I even hand over the credit card. I'm really hoping this won't last for too long. I'm thinking I'll work on this one with my therapist first...

Probably the most interesting to me as I reflect upon my actions and who I've become in these last ten days was my visit to the Christ Our Hope Catholic Church in downtown Seattle yesterday.

I was in Seattle to present on social media for small business. My return to work came after a week off to mourn and begin physical healing. No one told me I'd need time to heal. As a matter of fact, my doctor said I'd need maybe two days off from work. I am, at this point, certain that she has never personally experienced what I have experienced. While I hope and pray that she never does, I will be certain that she has the full scope and understanding of my experience to help her patients in the future. I took a full week and then trepidatiously began the return to my routine.

At the end of my first day in Seattle, reconnecting with some of my favorite colleagues from across the country, I found myself raw and empty. I love my colleagues and they wanted to offer me comfort but I do not know how to receive. I'm learning this. One of the reasons I love sharing on social media is because I can finally let people know through my own written word how I am really feeling. The raw, unfiltered truth. I can not do that face to face. I don't know the science behind it but I know it to be true. If I see you on the street I will smile and tell you I'm doing fine. I don't mean it but I can't handle the aftermath of telling you that I am suffering inside.

When people give me words of comfort on Facebook in comments and posts, and hundreds of my friends graciously have, I feel that comfort. I can absorb it. It is just as real and raw as my own sharing of emotion. Face to face I am incapable of handling the weight of those pure interactions. I am certain that somewhere along the line this disorder has a name but for right now the comfort that comes through my Facebook feed has been the purest and I think healthiest.

I lay there in my hotel room bed trying to curtail the panic of not having my husband's warm strong body next to me and I sought another form of comfort.

One of my colleagues was about to pass the anniversary of her wedding to her husband who was taken from her far too young. This was to be the first anniversary she would pass that she was not surrounded by family and that she was at work at all. I love this woman for her energy, brilliance and raw humor but in this moment I knew that her pain was right on the surface like mine. We had spent the evening eating chocolate delicacies and drinking cocktails while joking about her 14-year history as a Catholic school girl attending Jewish summer camps. She regaled us with her Jewish song knowledge. It occurred to me as I lay there in bed with my thoughts that perhaps a visit to church would give her some comfort. I wondered if it might comfort me as well.

I am fascinated by religion. All religion. I love being Jewish and at the same time have struggled with finding my own sweet spot in the faith. I watch movies and documentaries and read books and blogs all about different faiths as well as my own and have had some of my own most spiritual moments in a Mormon temple, a Christian prayer group, a Unitarian Universalist church as well as in many a synagogue around the world. I wondered what the experience of lighting a candle in a Catholic church might do for my own pain as well as for my friend's.

I sent her a Facebook message after doing a quick Yelp search to find the closest Catholic church in the vicinity of our event. I suggested a quick visit to light candles to honor the loved ones we were missing so deeply. And then I did what any Jewish girl in my situation would do: I laid there and felt guilty about it. Why, after all, did I not seek a synagogue to find some solace for my soul?

In watching many a television or movie scene filmed in Catholic churches of individuals lighting candles and then bearing their souls in individual prayer to God I could see where the action may bring some respite from pain. There really is no informal equivalent in my own practice of my faith. I would be lying if I did not tell you that I am very worried about writing these words as I do know there are some who will be uncomfortable with my feelings, but I believe in authenticity and these are my feelings from the depths of my being in all their authentic glory: I did not know how I could find the comfort I needed from my faith and, in all honestly I did not know that it could happen in a Catholic setting either. Either way, it seemed a better option than taking another drink.

I awoke the next morning with a message from my friend agreeing to meet me around noon at the church. I was nervous. It was a gloomy and cold day in Seattle. A huge contrast to the sunshine and warmth of the day before. I had not packed for the weather and knew a trip to Nordstrom Rack was in order. I caught a cab with another friend and we made a whirlwind tour through the store as I put together a presentation worthy outfit that would also keep me warm. The clerks checked me out in the dressing room and I walked out of the store wearing my new clothes.

My trusty Google Maps gave us the walking directions to the church just a few short blocks away. As we walked to the building to meet our Catholic friend, my mind started to fill with wonder about what I was about to do. Was I committing a sin? If so, in how many faiths? Did I really believe that God would punish me for reaching out for comfort, despite the venue? At the end of the day did it matter if, in some small way, I could quell the angst I was feeling?

We arrived at the address and found a Catholic services building. I noticed stained glass windows on the side of the building and surmised that the church must be within. We entered and a young man working behind the desk began to give me the history of the building and the services provided therein. My question to him was simply, "Is it okay if we go into the church and light a candle?" I love history. I love old buildings. I love services for the poor and marginalized, but this was not the time. My emotions were at the surface, my eyes were already wet with tears. Then the Father came out and the young man asked him if we could go in. I was nervous that he'd be able to figure out that we did not quite belong there. He was in a hurry and told us to "go talk to Diane she'll help you out and give you the..." And that's when I did it, I finished his sentence: "She'll give us the whole spiel?" Perhaps I was seeing something that didn't happen but

in that moment, after I unwittingly threw out a Yiddish term, he looked at me quizzically and pointed to the woman who was to help us.

With permission granted and blessings from Diane, the three of us became the perfect material for a bad joke. A red-headed Jew, a brown-haired Jew, and a blonde Catholic walk into a church... You know how it goes from there.

We approached the small section of candles placed under a three-dimensional image of the Virgin Mary. The candles were in neat rows in blue glass holders. Most were lit and burning peacefully, carrying the woes of others who had been there before. We took narrow wooden sticks and lit them with the burning flames. Mine seemed to burst with flame that quickly engulfed my stick. It was both funny and in a way appropriate in the moment. I quickly lit a candle and extinguished the stick. My friend took a seat in a pew and lowered the kneeling cushion. She crossed herself and silently began to pray and weep.

My red-headed friend and I took a seat in the row behind, lost in our own wave of emotions. My first thoughts were "Da lifnei mi atoh omed." A Hebrew phrase that means, "Know before whom you stand." During times of forced conversions, Jews for many centuries repeated those words in their heads while participating in group worship that was anything other than Jewish in nature. I've thought those words many times in my life.

Know before whom you stand.

Who was I standing before? From whom was I seeking comfort? I sobbed. My heart bled through my eyes. I had no conscious thoughts. I did not ask why. I did not moan, "why me?" I just sobbed. I was so sad and in such need for some sort of relief. The only time I can remember a similar sense of crying in prayer has been during my visits to the Western Wall of the Temple in Jerusalem, the Kotel. When I prayed there last in November of 2008, on my 36th birthday, I cried in pain, in questioning, in need for answers. These tears were different. There are no questions, the answer has already been delivered, my baby is not to be. So I simply cried.

I wish I could tell you that it was the magic cure-all I was seeking. That in the moment the flame leapt from the stick to the wick my aching heart was cured, the vast emptiness filling with love, but it didn't. It did, however, give me some time to quiet my soul, to cry for the sake of crying, to feel a connectedness to a higher being, to feel in unity with a friend.

I know my search for comfort will continue and I know that I will be able to choose avenues that are healthier than, say, drinking. I know this because now I've put it out there and at the very least my husband will be on the lookout. I also know now from my research that even though my pregnancy was not to term I still may suffer from postpartum depression, I have in the past, and I will seek the treatment I need to make it through to the other side. I will keep writing, and as long is it is helpful to you, I hope you will keep reading and letting me know you are there.

Most of all I will keep speaking to God in the ways I know and perhaps some more experiences I don't know. For, there is one thing I am indeed certain of, it does not matter how I communicate, in what language I reach out, where I am sitting or where a candle or prayer is said in my or my baby's name. A prayer is a prayer. Grief is grief. And comfort will come when comfort comes.

Monday, August 5, 2013

PLANTING A TREE TO REMEMBER

Today marks 2 weeks. 2 weeks since I saw the ultrasound image of my baby boy with no heartbeat. 2 weeks. I wonder how long it will take for me to stop counting. Perhaps it is because I had been so excitedly counting every day and week that my pregnancy advanced. Reading "The Peanut Report" to my husband from the many different apps on my phone. The kids asking me each week, "How big is Peanut now?" as he climbed from sweet pea to raspberry, to prune to lime, to peach, to orange. We were in the habit of counting.

The weight of the experience of losing our baby Peanut was crushing, and my husband was eagerly in search of ways we could lift the weight from our respected chests and gain some closure. I did not get to bury my baby. That is a loss that I don't know if I will recover from. We talked about creating a piece of artwork with the kids. We talked about putting some stepping stones in the garden. Nothing seemed like it would do much to ease our pain. Then we decided to plant a tree. I grew up getting "tree certificates" from family members for every happy occasion, and physically planting trees in Israel to create forests in the desert.

Planting trees has a strong connection to continuing life for me, and there is nothing more in the world that I have wanted during these weeks than to continue the life my son never got to live.

My husband and I went to the nursery in our neighborhood. They had several rows of trees just right for our arid climate. We touched each one and looked at their leaves. Which could be the tree to provide us with shade? Which would be just the right size to place a garden bench beneath? Which could provide a place for quiet reflection? Which could ease our pain? It was a tremendous amount to ask of a poor tree.

We settled on a European Mountain Ash. It would grow large enough to provide shade, but not too large as to encroach on our neighbor's lawn. It would produce a beautiful orange berry that would not harm our dog. It would grow tall (as every mother hopes her son will). Our younger children were at sleep-away camp, the eldest still away at Marine boot camp. We bought the tree and kept it on our back porch, awaiting the arrival of our two youngest so that together we could experience some sort of closure and continuation as a family.

Being pregnant at this stage of life, when my husband and I already have 3 beautiful children in our family, made the pregnancy very much a family affair. I had 4 sets of eyeballs watching my belly, watching what foods I ate, watching for growth and the development of the baby bump, asking about doctor's appointments and eager for the next ultrasound image we might bring home. They wanted to know anything and everything about their new sibling. All conversation was about their new brother and what life with him would mean.

We did not tell the kids that Peanut was no more while they were in the midst of their camping activities. As a matter of fact, our son in boot camp still does not know. We were hoping that by being prepared with a "closure plan" our 2 youngest children would be able to process more quickly and fully.

My 11-year-old came home first. He is an emotional child and makes very deep connections. When he first learned about his new brother to be he became very anxious that he would not be a "good role model." He worried that he would not be able to help him through life or to teach him how to cope with hardships as he has such trouble coping himself. He told me he was not sure that he was excited about the baby.

Each day we would talk through some of his fears and he, more than the others, kept a very close tab on how the pregnancy was going. He is anxious by nature, and this was a whole new thing to be anxious about. I dreaded telling him that we lost the baby. I knew he'd blame himself. I knew this to be a normal response for young children, especially for him. My husband and I worked on what we would say so that he would know, intellectually at least, that nothing he said or thought caused our baby to leave us. We decided upon: "Peanut is no longer with us. His little heart just could not make it. Even before we knew that I was pregnant, his little heart was not formed properly to make it to birth." I hoped that by adding the part about Peanut's heart not forming properly before we even knew I was pregnant that he would relinquish some of the guilt.

He was devastated. He cried. He sobbed. He held me very close. He told me about his plans for teaching Peanut. He told me how he was working hard to figure out a way to be the role model he wanted to be for his little brother. He gave me the mobile he had made in his nature clinic at camp for his baby brother. We showed him the tree that we began calling the "Peanut Tree" and he promptly transferred his anxiety to the tree worrying that it would die too.

Our 12-year-old daughter learned about Peanut a week later. In our first moment alone together I told her the same thing as I told her brother. She looked at me in shock. She did not believe me. When she realized it was true she said, "Wow, that is really depressing." She didn't cry. She is a completely different kid than her brother. I worried because she desperately wanted this baby. She had been asking me to get pregnant for years. I kept telling her it was not likely to happen.

Then, when I got pregnant she was over the moon with excitement. She wanted to buy little dresses and dolls and toys and furniture right away. She was certain it would be a girl. When she learned it would be a boy she asked if we could return him or exchange him for a girl. She was mostly kidding but I knew when she learned he was gone that she would feel guilty for those statements.

One day after learning her brother was gone my daughter stopped me as I was setting the table for dinner. Tears were already flowing from her eyes. She wrapped her arms around me and looked up at me - pain in every little freckle on her adorable face. "Mommy, did Peanut die because I was mean to you?" I know that intellectually she knew that wasn't possible. I also know that she has never been mean to me. Obnoxious as preteens can be? Yes. But mean, not a chance. I held her as she sobbed into my chest. My heart breaks for her pain, but I was grateful that she could hold me and cry and process. Both of the little ones home, the time had finally come to put the "Peanut Tree" into the ground. My husband cleared an area of our landscaping by moving bushes around and digging through the clay in our backyard. We were both raised in the Midwest where when you dig into the ground you are digging nice fertile dirt.

Here you dig clay and it always amazes us that anything can grow. We dug and marveled. My husband was covered in sweat and his muscles were working at maximum capacity. He was tired. It was hot. This was not fun. I wondered what was going on in his head.

The kids were helping to clear debris out of the yard and finally the time came to place the tree and fill the hole with dirt. My husband and I had talked about what this would look like. He wanted this to be a happy occasion. We were after all giving new life to a tree and making a happy place for all of us to remember Peanut. I was having a hard time and I worked very hard to hold back the tears. In the Jewish tradition, a funeral involves the loved ones of the deceased taking turns to shovel the dirt into the prepared gravesite. Often the dirt is lying on a tarp as we had the dirt prepared for planting. I have had experience in my life both participating and witnessing this process. It is considered the highest of gifts you can give to a person as nothing can be expected in return for this service.

As I watched my little son take shovel after shovel of dirt off of the tarp I tried mightily not to cry. This was not a funeral I kept telling myself. My son was not crying, he was simply taking the dirt and wanting to place it perfectly around the tree so that it would be stable and have the greatest chance of growing tall and strong. He looked at me and said, "I wanted to help my brother learn to grow and do this thing the right way." His voice trailed off and he kept shoveling.

My daughter took a couple of turns with the shovel before she just watched the rest, taking it all in. My husband, as he does with all things, took every placement of clay mixed with potting soil and compost into consideration to make sure all was level and the tree was planted as perfectly as could be.

And just like that, it was done.

The "Peanut Tree" is in the ground. It stands tall in its location just in the center of our backyard, visible from every window at the back of the house. Visible from my bedroom when I

wake up and visible from my living room windows which I can see as I wash dishes in the kitchen or lay on the couch watching TV or hanging out with the family.

It has not taken away my pain, foolish of me to think it could, but it may be a place to provide solace as it grows.

As we were cleaning up the tools to go inside a couple of rain drops fell on my skin. I looked over at the tree and caught a glimpse of my son gently stroking the trunk of the tree. Healing will take its own path for each of us. Perhaps this tree planted with love in memory of our Peanut will be a place for all of us to start.

Recovery

There are some things we may never understand

Thursday, August 8, 2013

Growing up, I spent many Saturday afternoons around the table with family and friends as the sun began to set, listening to stories of Elijah the Prophet. I always loved the Elijah stories which had been passed down generation to generation and made me think beyond the obvious. Elijah was always showing up in stories and helping the underdog and educating he or she who treated another unkindly. One of the stories that always sticks with me is the story of a man who meets up with Elijah and begs to join him on his journey.

"I just have to see how it happens and what you do." The man was very persistent. Elijah refused him repeatedly but finally gave in. "Okay, you can join me, but you can't ask ANY questions." The man agrees and off they go.

Dressed like beggars the two men approach a small shack of a house on the corner of a mostly barren field. In the field is a cow, not in much better condition than the field. Elijah walks up to the plank of wood acting as a door and knocks. An old woman opens the door.

"We are poor men just passing through. We have no money and are hungry and in need of a place to sleep."

The man traveling with Elijah looks past the old woman and sees a younger man sitting at the table. Two bowls have been set out and a quarter of a loaf of bread. He begins to wonder why Elijah would stop here, but remembers the rule: no questions.

The old woman welcomes the men into her home. She takes the bowls set out for herself and her son and invites the men to drink the broth and eat the bread. "We don't have much, but I can see we have more than you. In my home, you shall eat and rest and be ready for your travels in the morning."

The man followed Elijah's lead and ate the food, knowing he was taking food out of the mouth of the woman and her son. When the woman gave the men her cushions to sleep upon he knew that she, in turn, would sleep on the ground. But Elijah accepted the cushions, and he could ask no questions of Elijah. He slept a deep sleep.

Come morning, the woman gave the men the remainder of her loaf of bread and sent them out for their journey, wishing them well. As she closed the door Elijah asked G-d to make the cow ill until he died. At this, the man could not hold in his doubt and questions any further. "This woman gave you the food out of her mouth and the bed from beneath her body and you ask G-d to kill her cow?" He was shaking with anger. "How could you do that to her?"

Elijah looked at him and said, "No questions. Do you wish to continue with me?" The man took a deep breath and let out a long sigh. He nodded his head and the men began to walk again.

Still dressed as beggars, the men approached a castle aglow with candles. They could hear a party in full swing. As they got closer they saw a line of men and women dressed in fine silks with silver and gold draping their bodies entering the castle. The men joined the back of the line. Upon reaching the doors of the castle they were greeted by a man who gruffly asked them to leave the property, as they were not guests of the lord of the house.

"It is true, we are not guests of the lord of this house," Elijah began. "We are travelers seeking a place to lay our heads for the night and perhaps a bite to eat. Will you please summon your master so that we may beg of his protection for the night?" The servant, clearly perturbed by this ostentatious request, went to summon his master.

"Who comes here and disturbs my festivities?" The Lord demanded upon arrival. Elijah, bowing his head in deferential respect replied, "We are simply travelers in need of a place to rest for the night." The wealthy man began to laugh. "What, do you think this is, the village inn? This is my home, and I am entertaining this evening. I could not have you come in. Leave here at once."

Elijah turned to leave. Before he stepped off the top step he turned to the wealthy man and said, "I see you have a large hole in your outside wall." The man looked towards the hole, "Yes. We have been working to repair the hole, but the wall keeps refusing the patches." Elijah nodded knowingly. "May G-d help you to repair that hole and make the wall as strong as any wall that has ever been built." The homeowner simply looked at Elijah and turned his back on him, returning to his guests. The servant ushered Elijah and his companion from the property and admonished them to never return.

Well, at this point Elijah's partner was having fits trying to bite his tongue. He could not believe what he just saw. One who helped them graciously he cursed, and one who had all the means in

the world and would not even consider helping them he blessed? How could this be?? At the breaking point, he declares to Elijah, "Fine, I'm going home but you have to tell me why you would do these truly incomprehensible things."

Elijah pauses and considers the man's request. "Okay. If it will put your mind at ease I will explain, but then you must return to your home and leave me to my work." He continued, "The son of the old woman was about to become ill. His death would leave the woman with nothing, and she too would die soon after her son, broken-hearted and hungry. By asking G-d to take her cow, the son would be spared and could marry and bring wealth to the home."

The man began to understand. Elijah explained further, "The wealthy landowner we met had a wall that could not be repaired because behind that wall is a treasure 1,000 times more valuable than the wealth he already possesses. Had the wall not been repaired, the man would have become aware of the riches and surely a man who has so much and can't be bothered to help another should not be blessed with more."

The man left Elijah humbly realizing that all things are not what they seem. What may look like a curse may indeed be a blessing in disguise.

I don't know if I tell the story the same way as others, but this is how

I remember it. I have often thought of this story when things happen in my life and in our world that I can not understand. This story always pushes me to look for that unseen blessing that must lay under what appears to be such a painful curse.

Not much brings me peace as it relates to the death of our baby Peanut, but this story at least urges me to look for the peace.

Yesterday was my follow-up appointment with my OB following the D&C procedure, which was medically sound but emotionally traumatizing. For days, I had been preparing what I would say to her about the experience. I was going to implore her to never send another woman in my situation to that clinic. I was going to tell her how there needed to be a better way to care for women and their partners who experience fetal demise, those two words that rip a hole in my heart every time I see them.

I did not sleep the night before the appointment. I was nervous that I would not be able to keep my cool. I was worried I'd blow it. I feared that the muteness I experienced when I was in the clinic for my D&C would return.

I got out of bed the next morning and decided that I would print out the rough sketch of The Peanut Project, a program that I have begun to develop in memory of my Peanut to help women and their families in the 7 days immediately following miscarriage. I learned through my own experience that not much exists to help women and their partners get through the immediate needs and I believed we could help. I also printed every article I had written, from the excitement of finding out we were pregnant, to the devastation of learning Peanut had died, to planting a tree in memory of our little lost dream. I added some pictures of our family to make it as real as possible for her and ran to Office Depot to print it out. 47 pages later and spiral bound I felt confident that I would get through the experience and maybe help, at the very least, the women who come after me at this same practice.

My husband accompanied me to the appointment. The last time we sat in those plastic covered chairs, a short 2 weeks earlier, we were waiting to hear that Peanut was just fine. On this day we sat there, my stomach still bloated but my uterus empty. I could not help but feel envious of the other couples in the waiting room. Women with swollen uteruses in cute maternity clothing, their husbands holding their hands protectively. I felt like my heart was caving in and my breathing was very shallow. My husband kept trying to say things to make me laugh. He was anxious too.

We were finally called back to the room. First stop: the scale. I couldn't believe the number. No baby to blame anymore, at what would have been a 5 month check-up I'd packed on a whopping 20 lbs. 20 lbs? That's going to take me forever to take off...once I feel motivated again.

We entered the room and I sat on the table with my "Peanut Project" bound document in my hands. Each moment I waited I became more nervous. I just wanted to let her know, to educate her. In truth, I wanted her to come in and say it had all been a mistake, that the reason I was still so bloated was that I was still pregnant, that Peanut had a twin who managed to survive... I looked down at the document. The picture at the top of the page was that of my very first ultrasound. There, nestled to the top of my uterus, was the tiniest and cutest little baby just waiting to grow, a world of opportunity awaiting him. I remember the moment we first set eyes on him. We were smitten. He was not simply a fetus to us. He was our child and we loved him. We worried about him and had dreams for him, just as we do for our other 3 children. The doctor had not even entered the room and I was already crying. So much for the bravado.

I know from the emails I have received that some of you feel I need to find a new doctor or a new practice, but I stand by the fact that I have a great doctor. She came into the room and sat down with a caring loving look on her face. She wanted to know how I was doing. Like an anxious school girl answering the teacher in class, I just launched into it. My heart was pounding my body shaking. I told her about my completely unsatisfactory experience with my D&C. I told her that I should never have been sent to a clinic whose primary work is abortions. I told her that while they may have been adept at handling my medical needs, they were in no way capable of handling my emotional needs that were just as important at the time. I told her about the Peanut Project, and that through our experience we have learned how desperately women and their families need care and comfort and compassion in those first 7 days. I explained how there are not enough services available to meet those needs. I told her that care must start with her. I handed her the pamphlet.

I cried through all of it. My little baby Peanut was staring up at me from the paper in my hands. Tears fell onto the protective plastic cover.

My doctor just looked at me, devastation on her face. "I never would have wanted that for you. I am so sorry. I have not gotten feedback like that from any of my other patients." I wasn't surprised. It is excruciating to talk about. We don't want to talk about it. Maybe in some way, we feel like we deserve to be treated that way. We'd like to push the experience into a corner and hide it away for ever. Many of us remain silent.

I was sent for an ultrasound to alleviate my fears, and to check that the procedure had been performed correctly and that my uterus was clear. I laid on the same bed where 2 weeks before I had my last glimpse of Peanut as I watched the screen. Where once my uterus had been open and full with a baby growing, it was now a slim line on the screen nothing inside to make it blossom. My heart was heavy, but the tears gracefully stayed welled up in my eyes. It was true, Peanut was no longer there. The emptiness was heavier than anything I have ever felt before.

I don't ask G-d why. Like the man who followed Elijah so briefly, I know that I could never understand the answer. I can only take the gifts I have been given and make Peanut's life continue in an entirely different way.

Thursday, August 15, 2013

REACHING OUT AND BEING TOUCHED AFTER MISCARRIAGE

I have been quiet for the past week or so. My mind has a numbness I can't quite explain. I am no longer on the verge of constant tears. I can actually feel happiness and authentically laugh at funny moments. I can see myself on the horizon.

I woke up this past Friday morning with a heavier than usual feeling. I realized that through this process, I had not heard from any one of my siblings. My family, specifically my siblings, and I do not have the easiest path. Our closeness is awkward at best. While I'd heard daily from my mother and even received outreach from my step-mother and my father, it stung that I had not been reached out to by any of my 6 siblings.

Growing up as the oldest child, there was always a distance between myself and my siblings. My step-brothers were close in age but they had their own lives and their own challenges and a natural closeness never formed. My sisters are much younger than I at 10 and 18 years my junior. They formed a very close bond with each other and their lives followed a much different path than mine. My two brothers from my mother and father are 3 and 4 years younger than I and were always far more interested in torturing each other than in playing with me. But at the time he entered high school the brother 3 years my junior and I began to bond. We still have a very special bond. It includes passionate debate and arguing for each other's souls if you will, but at the end of the day, it is the one sibling relationship that has really stayed strong.

As he grew, my brother always insisted that while chronologically it did not add up the actuality was that he was older and wiser. This argument that he was my "older younger brother" kept up until I turned 40, at which point he said I could keep the title of older sibling. Over the past years, I have seen how he has indeed matured and grown and he has been the peace keeper in my family. I have been fortunate to have his love and support when I know it certainly has not been easy for him, or for any of my family.

When I woke Friday morning and realized that my unsettled feeling was linked to the fact that I had not heard from him I sent him a text. "I know you know I've had a miscarriage. I'm surprised I have not heard from you. I hope I have not done something to upset you." My brother does not like it when I text important stuff, yet he knows now that when I do it is because I do not have the strength to put a voice to my thoughts. To his credit, he called me within seconds of receiving my text.

As soon as I heard his voice I began to cry. I had not really cried for several days. I had even managed to get through several face-to-face conversations with friends without breaking down in a puddle of tears in the prior week. I believe it is because the emotion and history that ties siblings together are so strong that just hearing his voice brought all the emotions I had been working so hard to manage to the surface. His voice was like a hug that I so desperately needed even though I did not consciously realize it.

The reason he had not called was that he wanted to give me privacy. He did not know what to say or what I needed. He and his wife have been blessed, and may they continue to be, to not know of this experience firsthand. He figured I'd reach out when I needed him. And I did.

Much of my focus this past week has been on the Peanut Project and finding potential partners and volunteers on building out the program, as well as creating lists that can help families who are going through this. The feedback I keep getting, and that I have experienced first hand, is that we do not know how to talk about miscarriage. We, as a society, are uncomfortable with the loss of a child on such a scale that it induces a silence that runs very deep. The family who lost their pregnancy remains silent. Their family and friends remain silent. We look at each other with knowing, and those grieving are wished strength, but the hurt remains bottled up. It is only communicated through pain lines, lack of makeup and exhaustion wore like a mask on the faces of the bereaved.

I was honest with my brother about my pain. He listened and spoke words of comfort and care. It was painful and awkward and as soon as I could pull myself together I changed the subject. My brother and his family were on the way to Nebraska, bringing my brother closer to meeting the goal his older sister already achieved: visiting all 50 states. He's only got 3 more to go. I am so proud of him, as always.

I hung up the phone and felt vulnerable. I was not sure how I was going to make it through my day. My dear friend had invited a group of truly incredible women together for a brunch and spa day off from work in celebration of her milestone birthday. I did not want to bring the group down with the weight of my grief. I also did not want to miss out on celebrating with a woman I love and the amazing women she surrounds herself with. I put on my happy mask and sent her a text that warned her I was feeling a little vulnerable.

The brunch was delicious. Amazing what comfort food can do for a mood. Afterwards, we headed out to the spa. First stop - massage. I have not been a big massage girl. Most massages I have had have been related to physical therapy and it has been a painful, wincing, tear inducing experience. But I've heard the hype, and I know for many massage is a key to relaxation. This birthday celebration had been in the works for several months and originally I had planned to book a pregnancy massage but now I was no longer with child.

The masseuse came out. A gentle looking woman. Thin with shoulder length brown hair, warm brown eyes and an easy smile. She looked at me and asked if there were any special areas she wanted me to focus on. Her kindness opened me right up like a recent wound and I started to cry. "I was planning on a pregnancy massage, but I lost my baby 2 1/2 weeks ago." I was embarrassed for myself and mortified for her that she had to deal with such a basket case. She put her hand on my arm and said, "Don't worry, you've come to the right place. This is a safe space."

As I lay face up on the table, swaddled in warm blankets, she told me she was going to do a grief release process. She placed her scented hands on my scalp, one at the top of my head and one on at the base of my neck. She walked me through a meditative process meant to release the grief of my loss while retaining within me the soul of the baby who left my body too soon for me but just right for him. Her words comforted me and rang true to what my experience had been. Her voice was quiet yet strong. I cannot tell you exactly what she said, though I tried so hard to remember her words, but I can tell you they were just what I needed to hear. Tears streamed out of my eyes and down both sides of my face.

She finished the process and began a full-body massage. There were no more words, but the energy and strength that came from her hands filled my body and I felt renewed. I felt Peanut's soul inside of me. I felt his soul smiling. I felt his soul entwining with mine. I felt that I could carry him in me with joy, no longer bound to grief. I felt light. I have done energy work before, but I have never had an experience so transformative. I floated on that light feeling for the rest of the day, and a piece of it still helps me when the sadness creeps up and threatens to take over.

The Peanut Project is moving forward. One list we are dedicated to building is how to help people going through this process answer the question so many who wish to support their friends ask: "What may I do for you?" I learned after my massage that it was not an accident that I had the masseuse I did. The woman who arranged our spa day had been helped by this woman, as she too recovered from loss. She did not ask me what she could do for me, she just knew and she did it. Most of us, including those of us going through the painful loss, don't know how to have a conversation at all, let alone answer the question.

Here is what I have so far:

What may I do for you? People who are grieving may want/need the following. Offering these directly may be the biggest relief for a family:

Meals preparedPhone calls to loved ones madeAppointments created or cancelledChildcare for older childrenFruit basketsGift certificates to massage for a later dateA simple email or text message letting them know you are there and that you care

Starbucks deliveryA call from clergyA call from family with the simple statement: We know you are in pain. We hurt for you. We love you.

With your help, we can grow this list and help people comfort those who experience this loss, this early departure of a child so deeply wanted, whose presence, though fleeting, will leave an indelible mark.

Yizkor —Remembering the ones we've lost

SEPTEMBER 15, 2013

As I sat under the glistening tent I nervously fingered the blue Yizkor booklet a kind elderly volunteer handed to me moments before the service began. Yizkor is the public memorial service shared 4 times each year during significant Jewish holidays. As a child, I remember looking forward to Yizkor services because all who were not saying the prayer were ushered in to the hall. It was a break and as I got older I always hoped the young man I had a burning crush on would talk to me for a few minutes. He was tall, blonde, handsome, charming and I was madly in crush with him. His name was Michael. Not the same Michael I am married to today, but I always had a soft spot for boys with the name Michael. Even my first real boyfriend was named Michael, yet another in my line. But I digress. It is much more fun to talk about my Michael's then to remember the emotion I wish to share today.

As a child, I also remember that I played a very significant role following the Yizkor service. I was there to comfort my mother. My mother lost both of her parents within a year of one another. The first time you say Yizkor, and for many the only reason to say Yizkor, is to honor and raise up the spirit of the parents you have lost. I am so blessed to have all of my parents, but this year I lost one very dear to me. I lost my baby boy at 15-weeks gestation.

Monday. July 22nd. In the afternoon. I stared at the screen of the ultrasound machine as the kind woman running the machine with deep sadness in her voice said those words, the words that play over and over in my head, "Oh honey, I'm so sorry, there is his heart and it's not beating anymore." My own heart felt like it stopped beating at that moment and the weeks that have followed have been focused on grief, mourning, and learning how to move toward the future. Our story had taken a twist that I did not want to recognize.

This precise Saturday I sat under the tent was the Jewish holiday of Yom Kippur. It is the most revered holiday of all for many in the Jewish faith, as it signifies the culmination of the year behind us. We pray for forgiveness of the wrong doings of the year past, we take stock in a year well lived, or a year we may have done more with. We reflect on all that happened to us and we hope, in unison as a community around the world, that each of us shall be inscribed in the book of life for a year of piety, progress, and plenty. It is also a day which for many in the Jewish community a 25 hour fast – no food, no water, no substance passing your lips – is observed. It is a solemn day.

I have always loved this holiday because on this day 30 years ago, my first sister was born. It was, until that point in my young life, the best thing that had ever happened to me. I celebrated the day and even today felt joy remembering what a blessing came to the earth on a Yom Kippur another life time ago.

8 weeks. 8 weeks ago, I was full of joy and anticipation. Today I sat empty. My body has begun to return to a pre-pregnancy shape, but my heart remains shattered and empty, longing for the little baby growing inside of my body. I have been seeking a closure of sorts. I have been seeking a way to feel that I have honored my son as a member of my family who is respected and who has made an impact, just like his brothers and sister. I decided that saying the Yizkor prayer would help me elevate a soul whose physical presence was felt solely by me.

Before the holiday, I agonized about whether my participating in the prayer was disrespectful in some ways to my parents and the others in the service. I know that so many women have suffered the loss of a pregnancy, and I knew of no others who had participated in the ritual of Yizkor. Was I making a mockery of the prayer? I agonized over my decision all the way until the Rabbi began to prepare us for the service. I figured to myself that no one knew for whom I was saying Yizkor and it could be a personal private moment. That was, until the Rabbi asked us to take a few moments to turn to our neighbors and share a special memory we had of the person or people for whom we were reciting the prayer. I began to panic.

The people in my row began to share about their parents long gone, their spouses who had passed too young. The woman next to me lost her spouse the year I was born. Everyone in the row had spoken and my neighbor turned to me. "Who are you reciting the prayer for, dear?" I looked at them, grateful for an outdoor service providing me the opportunity to hide behind my sunglasses, and started to speak.

"This is my first time saying the Yizkor..." was all I could get out before I began to sob. The group began to comfort me, telling me it would get easier and all I kept thinking was that they did not know why I was here and would they feel I was less than, or did not belong here. I had chosen this service to attend on purpose. The gathering of community was brought to the Denver Botanic Gardens by Judaism Your Way. Their mantra: 'Wherever you are on your Jewish journey, we will meet you there.' I knew that I was welcome by the organizers to say whatever prayers I needed to say to heal, but how would the "congregants" feel?

I gathered myself together enough to finish my sentence. "I'm here to say Yizkor for the baby I lost just shy of 8 weeks ago." I was shaking, the chest shaking that happens when I am trying so desperately to hold back the sobs. It occurred to me that I had not cried about losing my baby in over 2 weeks.

The women in the group looked at me with deep caring and concern, half-smiles of knowing on their faces. The man asked me what the baby's name was. I was almost embarrassed to tell them. Since I did not have the opportunity to bury my baby because of the way my procedure was handled, I never gave him a name. I answered shyly, "We called him Peanut." I had so much I wanted to share about this baby I loved and wanted so desperately, but all I could get out was to share a dream I recently had about him. In this dream, I had died and for the first time I met Peanut. He was an adorable and happy little boy. He came up to me and hugged me and then, the first words out of his mouth, "Ma, Peanut? Really? You couldn't come up with a better name?" He was definitely a child of mine!

We all had a nice chuckle and then the women in the group shared their own pregnancy loss experiences. They too had been there, or their parents had. They comforted me. They welcomed me. And as I sobbed through the words of the prayers, I knew that I was safe to pray for peace for the little soul who left too soon.

One prayer we read from the prayer book On Wings of Awe was particularly poignant for me:

"It is hard to speak of oneness when our world is not complete, when those who once brought wholeness to our life have gone, and naught but memory can fill the emptiness their passing leaves behind.

But memory can tell us only what we were, in company with those we loved; it cannot help us find what each of us, alone, must now become.

Yet no person is really alone; those who live no more echo still within our thoughts and words, and what they did has become woven into what we are.

We do best homage to our dead by living our lives fully even in the shadow of our loss. For each of our lives is worth the life of the whole world. In each one is the breath of the Ultimate One.

In affirming the One, we affirm the worth of each one whose life, now ended, brought us closer to the Source of Life, in whose union no person is alone and every life finds purpose."

As I read the words, "We do best homage to our dead by living our lives fully even in the shadow of our loss." I understood what I must do and the marching orders I have. Throughout the services in this beautiful tent surrounded by the waterfalls and flowers of the vast gardens an orange and black butterfly flitted in and out around my seat. A message, perhaps, from Peanut that all is well and beautiful for him and will be for me as well.

Yizkor. I remember the feeling of his presence in my body. I remember the excitement and ecstasy of seeing his little heartbeat on the screen. I remember how he waved to us and hiccuped during his ultrasound appointment. I remember the sheer joy he brought to me, his father, his siblings and to all who learned about his existence. I remember and hold strong the love and connection we forged as he grew inside of me. In honor of his memory I move forward, I seek joy and I work to make an impact.

The golden ring in the cycle of loss

April 25, 2014

One year ago, I walked out of the sliding glass door in my kitchen to take stock of the situation with our Aspen trees. Barely saplings, my husband and I had planted the trees the summer before and I was not confident they would thrive. They were tall and thin. The branches looked as if they would never survive the raging drought that lasted through the winter months. As the Spring thawed the ground, I looked each day in hopes that little buds would form and prove that life still existed inside the stalks of the trees. I approached the trees, standing and swaying like three old weeds waiting to be pulled, and there I saw it, little splashes of green as their leaves began to release themselves from their slumber. Rebirth. Just moments before I had stared with awe as the pregnancy test showed me two lines indicating a spring was happening deep inside of me as well.

Today I saw it again, the first sign of the leaves exploding out of the somewhat stronger Aspen trees. But today, I sat in my chair at the kitchen table looking out through the glass doors and didn't venture outside to see. It has been quite a year. Excitement as the baby grew inside of me and the entire world bloomed as well, and then darkness as our baby died in my womb and left my body just shy of 20 weeks after our journey together began.

I processed.

I wrote.

I cried.

I screamed.

I grieved.

I mourned.

I shut down.

And then, I found purpose. I knew that the way my husband and I experienced this loss and the inadequate care we received following was wrong. If it was happening to us, it was surely happening to others. Something had to be done, and my husband and I were the ones to do it. We started The Peanut Project to support others by creating new norms for dealing with pregnancy loss and family support in the way we wish we had been supported.

I got to work.

I found purpose.

I re-learned how to smile.

Most of the time I was okay. And yet, I would wake up crying for my baby. I had very vivid dreams of my son. I saw signs of him everywhere, from a peanut shell showing up in my mint plant to the abundance of mother/baby images that I enountered in my day to day interactions. He was with me.

I was desperate to be pregnant again, and I kept eating for two. My body never stopped looking pregnant. It taunted me. Each month I was sure I had conceived. I felt traditional early pregnancy symptoms like nausea, fatigue, and a heightened sense of smell and each month as I counted the days of my cycle my period came. As my weight continued to climb, the close of each monthly cycle ripped at my uterus and tore through my spirit. And I ate, and ate. I ate to feel joy. I love a good meal and my husband is an unbelievable cook. We nurtured our souls with food. Meanwhile, I was ravaging my body.

My friends who have watched me work so hard to maintain a healthy body weight as a means of controlling the diabetes that is always threatening to explode within me gently supported me. My husband tip-toed around the issue, wanting me to know that he loved me and desired me as a man desires a woman, no matter what my body looked like. He silently feared for my wellbeing as he saw me fall exhausted in to bed each night well before the children.

I knew I was not okay, but I did not know what to do about it. I also did not really want to do anything about it. I was doing alright enough. I was doing my work. I was getting through the days. I was trying to build my business. And with each step of the day-to-day, I told myself I was doing okay and I had recovered from the loss. Then I had a fight with my husband.

Michael and I hardly ever fight. We disagree, and sometimes it takes a bit of effort to hear each other out and come to an agreement (meaning he finally agrees to see it my way), but it is a rarity for us to fight. It was a silly argument over a very inconsequential interaction, but I was hurt and then he was hurt. Eventually it exploded into a torrent of tears and his honest proclamation that he was scared for me, scared for the health of my mind and my body. Then he said the words that sent my heart to the depths of sadness: he "wanted his wife back."

The following morning I was celebrating with a friend who was recovering from cancer on her 40th birthday. We went to a spa for the day with a group of her close friends. As I was chatting with one of the women, I heard myself say what I'd said hundreds of times since the loss of the baby, "I don't want to lose the weight, it's the last thing I have of the baby." As the words came out I realized it was time. I realized that I could not eat my way back to being pregnant with my son. I realized that no amount of pounds added would equal pregnancy. I knew my husband was right; his wife was gone and only I could bring her back. I did not realize that I had buried myself with the baby I never got to physically bury.

I made two calls. The first was to my nutritionist. The second was to a counselor, a friend and colleague who came very highly recommended. It was during our second session that I had an experience like none other before.

I sat in the middle of the long couch on the crack between the cushions as she sat in her chair. I was admiring her beautiful Spring outfit and was full of angst about what we might address, the baby or any of the other challenges I seemed to be facing. She asked me what I'd like to address and I said, "the challenge I am feeling with my step-son." Home on 10 days of leave before deploying to Japan for 3 years of military service, he had seemingly regressed to his high school behaviors. He was treating the family with disrespect and I did not know how to handle my feelings about it. It was present and I felt impacting my ability to focus on the healing I needed to do.

She asked me to close my eyes, my feet firmly planted on the ground and my body supported by the pillows behind me. As memories flowed in my mind's eye, she asked me to focus and let her know when the stream stopped. As each one flew by tears began to drip down my face and my memories came to a rest. I knew where I was.

I was laying on a table. I was in a hospital. It was silent. I was alone except for the presence of a blue baby in between my legs. I had just given birth, but the baby was silent. I was calm and there above me was the spirit of my daughter. She was checking me out. She was deciding wether she was going to join us in this world or continue on her journey. Her spirit was pleasant, warm and loving - all the things she is today even at 13-years-old. In a way all her own she smiled and decided she'd join us. It was the instant between her entrance in this world and the entrance of 30 doctors and nurses as a code was called and my first-born baby revived.

My memories began to move again flying through my grandmother's house and coming to rest once more on a picture of my husband that hangs on our staircase. I remembered it as the first picture I ever saw of him. He appeared to be in a wooden room. He was sitting and wearing his favorite green sweater. His face was glowing and his body appeared to be made of light and energy. The energy began to fill my body and my mind moved once more. This time I felt pain.

It was ripping through the back of my head, a searing pain that began to pull me back. My counselor asked me to describe what I was feeling. I focused on the pain and felt a ring attached at the base of my neck wrapped through my cerebral cortex, controlling me. The ring pulled at me, and my breath was being taken away by the control it had over me. Once again my counselor guided me. She asked if any of the people in my memories could help to release me from that ring. I focused on all of the people I had seen: my husband, my daughter, my grandmother. Finally, help seemed to come from Peanut, my baby that was never born, he was pulling on the ring.

At first I thought he was there to help. Tthen I realized he was yanking on the ring. I wanted him to stop, to let go. I focused on asking him to stop controlling the ring to let me go and as this struggle was going on in my mind and the tears were flowing through sobs I had a window, a moment of clarity. Peanut was not controlling the ring; I had put the ring there to tether his spirit to mine. While his physical presence had left my body, I was holding on with all of the might I could summon to his spirit. Fear and panic wracked my body as I knew I had to let his spirit be. I had to let him go and do and be whatever he is to be in this world and that by tethering him to me I was preventing both of us from giving to the world what it is that we are here to give.

Knowing I was holding him back helped me want to release him, but the idea of separating his soul from mine felt like having the D&C to remove his body from mine all over again. I focused on the pulling at the back of my head and silently spoke to him as I had when he was growing in my womb. I told him I was excited for him to go out and perhaps be born to another. I wondered what he might do in this world, and I wished I could watch him and see him manifest in another's baby. I assured him

I'd be okay and that he could go and I would no longer keep him tied to me. Together we began the process of separation, a separation that should have happened months earlier.

I left my counselor's office with so many emotions. A special closeness to my daughter, a respect for the energy that my husband brings to us and a sense of wonder for who or what Peanut may now become.

When I woke from a very deep sleep the next morning my body was overcome by the emotional journey of the day before. I spent the day in bed only noticing the budding leaves on the Aspen trees as I came downstairs to sit at the table for dinner. I sat there at peace, surrounded by my family and surrounded by their love which continues to support me on my journey.

Today

I've learned that we are lacking systems to help people in our position. We lack them not for an absence of caring. We lack for the simple fact that this is a very hard reality to deal with, and most people are at a total loss, family as well as friends and loved ones, when something like this happens.

Here are some ideas of what you can seek out in your community. If they don't exist, I encourage you to lead the way to creating these or any of your own ideas to support our families.

1. Help with scheduling of next appointments such as D&C.

2. Call a clergy member if they are connected to one. Offer to find a clergy member of their preferred faith if not connected and interested.

3. Provide information on fetal burial if interested and make requested arrangements.

4. Help to begin a food chain from their physical community surroundings to support the family from the moment of call up to 7 days following the D&C.

5. Provide leads to support services for other children in the family.

6. Make calls to additional family members as requested by the family.

DOCTORS/MEDICAL PROFESSIONALS:

Work with medical providers to provide them with the information about the emotional needs of their patients who may experience fetal demise.

Families should feel supported and get the help they need immediately following the diagnosis of fetal demise. This also helps the medical provider to transition the patient from the shock of the news to the ability to take the next steps needed for their care.

CLERGY:

Reach out to the houses of worship and develop relationships with faith communities who would be willing to support families in need through the development of a volunteer committee within their church manned by families who have also experienced miscarriage and would be willing to be the organizers of food services for the families in need.

Create a list for a connection to individuals who request support who are not already formal members of a faith community.

BURIAL SERVICES:

Check with the funeral homes and burial service providers to learn the steps needed to be able to offer help to a family who may request this when burial is an option.

NON-FAITH BASED SERVICES:

Seek out volunteers who will be available to talk about and develop a non-faith based experience to provide closure to a family suffering from this sudden loss.

Dafna Michaelson Jenet
This evening was hard. Tomorrow is 1 week. I was writing and sobbing into Michael's chest trying to be quiet about it so as not to stress my boy. He comes over and tells me to imagine Peanut happy and playing with kids in the park. Such a great attitude. Then he made me watermelon art or rather, heart. So grateful for the men in my life, large and small. — with **Michael Jenet.**
JULY 28, 2013 NEAR HENDERSON, COLORADO

111   14 Comments

👍 Like   💬 Comment   ↪ Share

Losing a baby is not something we get over alone. It is our job to be a community to those who suffer loss. To be present, to offer a shoulder to cry on, an ear to listen, and our strength when the bereaved no longer have any reserve of their own. By sharing our stories, we lift the veil of silence that shrouds loss and we allow our families and communities to heal. I encourage you to share your stories, to speak openly about loss and to encourage those who suffer in silence to no longer be held prisoner by their sadness and fear. Together we can build healthy communities where recovery happens and families thrive.

CPSIA information can be obtained
at www.ICGtesting.com
Printed in the USA
BVOW09s0140160318

510638BV00005B/9/P

9 781628 654424